CLIMBING THE LADDER

Yours faithfully
David Barr

CLIMBING THE LADDER

THE STRUGGLES AND SUCCESSES
OF A VILLAGE LAD

AUTOBIOGRAPHY

OF

DAVID BARR

𝕷𝖔𝖓𝖉𝖔𝖓

ROBERT CULLEY

25-35 CITY ROAD AND 26 PATERNOSTER ROW, E.C.

Published for the Author

FIRST EDITION . . . *April* 1910

TO THE MEMORY OF

MY SAINTED MOTHER

WHO BY HER FORTITUDE AND CHRISTIAN CHARACTER

ILLUSTRATED THE BEAUTY OF GOODNESS AND THE

INESTIMABLE VALUE OF TRUE RELIGION

IN A LIFE BESET WITH

MANY DIFFICULTIES AND TRIALS

FOREWORD

RELUCTANCE to appear in print, consciousness of a want of the requisite literary talent, and the multitudinous activities of a busy career, have withheld me for years from yielding to the request of many friends to publish the story of my life. The evening of life has, however, brought me the opportunity, and my scruples have been overborne by the argument that the narrative may prove an encouragement and stimulus to some lad who has to struggle with poverty and difficulties in his effort to clamber up the difficult and rugged steeps of life.

These chapters contain nothing but the plain, unvarnished annals of an eventful course, overruled by the Providence of God. They have been written, not for self-exhibition, but to the praise of Him whose goodness and guidance have been so manifest all through the strenuous years of a long existence.

'Inverness,'
  Birmingham,
    February 1910.

CONTENTS

LIST OF ILLUSTRATIONS

CLIMBING THE LADDER

CHAPTER I

EARLY DAYS

'Home of my childhood! loveliest spot on earth!
How bright, how dear, how sad, the thoughts
That linger round thee—that sketch with clear and
Vivid lineaments the scenes of bygone years!'
(From Prize Poem, written 18—.)

I OPENED my eyes on the world on March 18, 1831, in a scattered hamlet appropriately called Wood End, a mile distant from the village of Fillongley, and not far from the home of 'George Eliot.' It is now a purely agricultural district; but in the days of my childhood—when hand-looms were in fashion—ribbon-weaving was a common occupation in the cottage homes of that neighbourhood. The silk was fetched from warehouses at Coventry, six miles distant, and returned when converted into ribbons. By this occupation the wives of farm labourers were able to eke out the poor pittance of their husbands. The condition of agricultural labourers was very hard and sad:

13

the hours were long, and the average wage, except in harvest-time, did not exceed eight or ten shillings per week ; while in many cases they were forced to be idle on wet days, unless indoor work happened to be available. Threshing-machines were not then invented, and wheat and other grain had to be beaten out with the flail. The monotonous thud of that implement was one of the familiar sounds all through the winter months. Scythe and sickle have been superseded by mowing-machine and reaper, and many other mechanical innovations have revolutionized agriculture as well as manufacture. Within my recollection marvellous transformations have taken place on every hand through the advance of science, often creating acute industrial problems. In my youthful days lucifer matches were unknown. I have visions of my father sitting up in bed with his nightcap on his head, striking flint and steel to get a spark into the tinder-box. If the tinder happened to be damp the process was tedious, and a considerable time elapsed before he succeeded in producing a spark sufficient to ignite a brimstone match.

The railway system was in its infancy, and the carriages were most crude and uncomfortable. I retain a vivid recollection of a journey on a cold winter's night, when I had to stand in a railway carriage that had no covering whatever, and bear the full force of storm and cutting wind. Those who were fortunate enough to secure a seat sat back to back down the centre in 'knife-board' fashion. First-class passengers were favoured with the protection of a roof, on the top of which their luggage was piled and covered with tarpaulin. The guard's seat also was on the outside, at the front end of the carriage.

In those days it was a luxury to ride, and the rule was to walk. I had experience of this on one occasion while quite young, when I walked from Leicester to my home—a distance of twenty-eight miles—in one day. On another occasion I had to walk to Birmingham, seventeen miles, to catch the six o'clock morning train. We seem to be losing the art of walking in these degenerate days, and expect a tram-car or omnibus to be provided for the shortest distance.

In the days of which I am writing it was a common thing to see the notice, 'Parish House,' painted over a cottage door here and there. Instead of placing the necessitous poor together in one large building, cottages were bought or rented by the guardians to provide free shelter for those in need—a custom which I believe dates from 1547, and continued until about the year 1834, when Union workhouses for paupers began to come into existence.

I find in searching the parish register that my family have lived in the locality of Fillongley for nearly two hundred years; but I have no trace of where my ancestors hailed from when they settled in that neighbourhood. The name suggests

Scottish extraction. For a considerable period it assumed the form of 'Barrs,' but originally it appears to have been as now spelt.

My parents were united in marriage on June 14, 1814, and commenced their life in very humble circumstances. My father was a country shoe-maker, dependent for his trade chiefly on people of the working class; and my mother, for some time after marriage, supplemented his earnings by ribbon-weaving. In the course of a few years they had to provide food and clothing for eight children, which severely taxed their resources. To com-plicate matters, before their children were old enough to earn a living, they began to attend a Nonconformist place of worship near to their home. This aroused a feeling of bitterness and persecution; my father was boycotted in his trade, and he sacrificed certain charitable gifts which were withheld from all who attended chapel. The patronage of Church people being withdrawn, he had to look further afield for support, travelling week by week to Coventry and other places, miles distant, in search of orders. He was a most indus-trious and hard-working man, but suffered for years from an inward affliction, which added to the hardships of his life. He lived nevertheless to a ripe old age.

My mother was a woman of beautiful, exem-plary, and heroic character, whose influence did much to mould my life and has followed me all through the intervening years. Though battling

BIRTHPLACE

with poverty and the many difficulties involved in rearing a large family, she was resolved not only to live honestly and pay twenty shillings in the pound, but to do something if possible to improve the circumstances in which we were placed, and to provide as far as she was able for the future welfare of her children. To accomplish this she exercised the most rigid thrift and economy, and trained her family to do their utmost to attain the object she had in view. From early years each was required to render help in various ways in the development of her plans. In the garden my task was to dig and hoe the ground, and to cut the grass by the side of the paths with a table knife —special implements being beyond the limited means of my mother, who always, with the full consent of my father, acted as family cashier. In the house I was requisitioned to clean knives, boots, and furniture, or to fulfil any other domestic duty of which I was capable.

In course of time my father was able to buy a pony and trap, and keep two or three cows. This enlarged the scope of my youthful employment, for I had now to groom and feed the horse, tend the cattle, and clean the conveyance. On butter-making days it was my work to turn the handle of the churn, sometimes a tedious and wearying process. When the butter was slow in forming, local superstition attributed this to Satanic influence, and a halter was fastened round the churn to break the spell and expedite the butter.

During harvest-time my father sometimes contracted with a neighbouring farmer to reap a field of wheat with the sickle, and those of his children who were able were called upon to assist in executing the work. These were days when the ancient custom of gleaning was permitted. This began as soon as the last sheaf was gathered. Occasionally a kind-hearted farmer allowed us to commence gleaning while the corn was being carted. A considerable stack of wheat, barley, and oats was accumulated by our united efforts, and in due time was hand-threshed and winnowed; the wheat being sent to the mill to be ground into flour for the family, the oats reserved for the pony, and the barley for the pig.

Excursions were made for the purpose of gathering mushrooms, hazel-nuts, cowslips, and anything else that might be lawfully appropriated. These were sent to market and converted into cash, partly to help the maternal exchequer and partly as a perquisite for the children. With money so saved I was enabled to purchase a black-faced sheep, which in due time brought forth two lambs, when I began to think I was getting rich. These may seem trifling and commonplace incidents, but they played an important part in forming my habits for future life, and I have often felt thankful for the valuable lessons in care and economy which they instilled.

It frequently fell to my lot to follow the example of my namesake of old—the psalmist

David—and take my father's sheep and cattle to graze in the green lanes, tending them from morning till night. A good deal of wayside pasture was available in days before the Enclosure Act had given power to adjoining landowners to annex considerable areas that abutted on their property. I often felt it to be a dreary and monotonous occupation; and when I had to approach what was known as 'Hobgoblin Lane,' ghostly phantoms seemed to confront me and haunt me with gloomy apprehensions. I usually filled up the long hours of these days in searching for birds' nests, sometimes mischievously transferring the eggs from one nest to another, chasing butterflies, shooting birds with a catapult, dreaming dreams, building castles in the air, and earnestly longing for manhood, when I should do what I pleased and not what I must.

CHAPTER II

EDUCATION

'A boy is better unborn than untaught.'—*Gascoigne.*

AT an early age I was put to a Dame's School, which must have been near my home; but I have no distinct recollection of this step. Very little learning could result from this experience, and therefore it can scarcely be taken into account. My real school-days commenced when I was seven years of age, and continued till I was twelve. The school was situated at Fillongley, and was conducted in a large irregular-shaped room over several parish houses. In one of these single-roomed cottages my father's widowed sister lived, and it was my practice to go and sit with her while I ate my dinner, which I took with me in a little cotton bag. The master was a quaint-looking man about fifty or sixty years of age, stout and podgy, having a very large head, and standing only about four feet six inches high. He had a soft and flabby hand, but could use it to purpose in applying a holly-stick to the palms of defaulting pupils. He was supported by an assistant teacher, who performed his duties fairly well, and always with a single eye! The whole of the instruction imparted was comprehended under the 'Three R's': I do not remember that I ever received a lesson in grammar during the whole time spent at school. Indeed, I question if the master himself was competent to give instruction in a subject which was quite outside the curriculum of village schools in those days. It will be easily understood, therefore, that all the education I obtained was of a very rudimentary kind.

I was fond of my school work, and attached great importance to it. In my simplicity I often made it the subject of my prayers, that I might acquit myself satisfactorily and derive all possible advantage from my limited opportunities. The school being endowed by an ancient charity, my education never cost my parents a penny beyond a small outlay in books, which were very few and inexpensive. Some of the poorest boys were provided with jackets, caps, and breeches—some blue, others green—at the expense of another charity provided by a benevolent individual in the days of long ago. Morning school was opened with the reading of a portion of Scripture, and once a year the scholars were taken to the parish church, and, standing in a line up the aisle, were publicly catechized in the presence of the congregation by the vicar, who occupied the pulpit or lectern. In riper years my soul revolted against the teaching of baptismal regeneration which was then inculcated;

B 2

yet on looking back on those exercises I am bound to confess that on the whole they exerted a beneficial influence on my character. Even such teaching is preferable to a purely secular code that would exclude the Bible and religious instruction altogether.

On leaving Fillongley school at the age of twelve I had a great desire for further tuition; and my mother, who was now in a rather better financial position, took me to Dr. Sheepshanks, Principal of Coventry Grammar School, but finding that the fees were beyond her means we returned home with sad hearts. Instead, therefore, of pursuing my studies I was compelled to leave home to earn my living, as narrated in a future chapter. The trade I had chosen for myself was printing, thinking that in such a vocation I should have free access to books, as I had not the means to purchase them; but the gratification of this desire also was denied me.

During my school days, and afterwards, I embraced every opportunity to improve my mind and add to my slender attainments. I had a taste for drawing, but no master to teach me, nor money to obtain materials. To overcome the latter difficulty my mother allowed me the white paper in which she bought her tea and other goods; but to enforce a useful lesson I was required to wind so much worsted, or render some other service, as payment for the same. The paper so earned I ironed out to remove the creases, and then bound into books, by the aid of which I trained myself in the art of pen-and-ink sketches and water-colour paintings, my favourite subjects being birds, animals, and houses. Some of these home-made drawing-books are still in my possession and remind me of the difficulties of my early life.

Another ambition which seized me in those days was to acquire the art of shorthand writing, but here again not one of my friends could render me the slightest assistance. I managed, however, to buy *Odell's System*, and by diligent study and practice was at length proficient enough to report a good portion of a sermon. There were no evening schools, mutual improvement classes, or public libraries within reach. The nearest facilities of this sort were at a Mechanics' Institute, but as it was situated six miles distant it was of no practical advantage. After commencing work as a shoemaker, at the immature age of thirteen, I began taking lessons of a village schoolmaster, two miles away; but this was vetoed by my employer, who often required me to work till a late hour, and to my great regret it had to be abandoned.

It will be seen that my opportunities were not commensurate with my thirst for mental improvement. The hours of labour were much longer then than now, and I had to work early and late. Bank holidays were not instituted, early closing was undreamed of. What would I not have given for the privileges enjoyed by the youth of the present day! Much of what little I know has been acquired since my school days. In this connexion I would record that I subsequently derived great advantage from my association with a Young Men's Improvement Society connected with the place of worship which I attended as a young man. I took an active interest in its work, and ultimately became its secretary. It was a vigorous and influential institution, and some of its members rose to positions of usefulness and eminence as ministers and local preachers, the training and help they received in this class no doubt largely contributing to their advancement.

Another element in my early training, for which I always feel the greatest obligation, was the influence of my employer, into whose service I entered at the age of seventeen, and in whose home I lived for some years during the formative period of my life. A green, uncultured youth, I was entirely unfitted for the important post he gave me, but with all the patience, forbearance, and extreme kindness of an intimate friend he bore with my incompetence and ignorance. The instruction and discipline of character received at his hands did perhaps more than anything else to equip me for the duties of my after life. Of this more in a future chapter.

CHAPTER III

THE SOUL'S AWAKENING

'A charge to keep I have,
   A God to glorify;
A never-dying soul to save,
   And fit it for the sky.'

IT has been a matter of life-long gratitude that I was led to give my heart to God in early life, when between eleven and twelve years of age. It came about in this way: My mother's example and influence had made an impression on my mind for good, but the experience of converting grace did not take place until near the end of 1843. The Rev. Thomas Collins was appointed to the Coventry Circuit, and commenced his ministry in September of that year. He visited Wood End in his turn, and the little chapel was close to my father's house. It was his custom to arrive in the afternoon, and fill up the interval until service in visiting the members of Society, afterwards going from house to house inviting every one to the service, giving them a word of Christian counsel, and then kneeling down to pray. It fell to my lot to pilot him in his pastoral visitation, and on the way he embraced the opportunity of entering into serious conversation with me about my spiritual state. He was a man mighty in prayer, who lived in close union and fellowship with God. On his journeys from Coventry to Wood End it was his wont to turn aside into a retired spot, where he poured out his soul in supplication and sought equipment for his work. Thus baptized with power from on high, no wonder his preaching found its way to the conscience and hearts of his hearers.

Under his ministry a very blessed revival swept through the circuit, and I was one amongst many others who found the Saviour. The arrow of conviction pierced my soul, and for some time I was in great distress, groaning for deliverance from the burden of sin. I could go to-day to places where secretly, under hedgerow or some other secluded spot, I retired to plead with God for pardon. My unhappy condition continued until one Sunday morning, when I went to the seven o'clock prayer-meeting. Falling on my knees in much sorrow I pleaded with God in the lines of one of the penitential hymns in the early part of the hymn-book of that date, and when so engaged light and peace and heaven came into my soul, and I arose from my knees happy in God. The blessed assurance of His pardoning love made me leap for joy, and everything around me seemed bright and beautiful. The little Bethel where I found the blessing was a very plain and unadorned building ; the congregation sat to hear the Word on rude benches that had no backs to them, males one side, females the other; the hymn was given out two lines at a time; everything was of the most primitive character. Yet, the simplicity and unattractiveness of the surroundings notwithstanding, I dearly loved the place where I found the pearl of great price, and from that day forward it was a joy to me to light the fire in the stove, sweep the floor, or top with snuffers the tallow candles by which the chapel was lighted—occasionally, to my dismay, snuffing out the light in the pulpit altogether! Young people to-day crave for entertainment; I found ample satisfaction in the service of this simple village chapel. To me it was the House of God and the very Gate of Heaven. I felt great delight, as well as profit, in the early Sunday morning and week-night prayer-meetings, the class-meeting and public worship; and occasionally I walked six or seven miles, to Coventry or elsewhere, to get a morning service.

There being no service in the forenoon it became a common practice for a band of praying men and women to visit surrounding villages and hold prayer-meetings in the cottages of well-disposed friends. The cause thrived, and two Society Classes were formed, three or four of whose members became local preachers.

On one occasion Mr. Collins met these classes for renewal of tickets, and it so happened that at that visit the leaders did not appear to be in a very vigorous state.   In answer to the usual question at such times, 'How are you getting on ?' one leader replied in desponding tones, whereupon Mr. Collins stopped him; 'Halliday! Halliday!' he exclaimed, 'have you nothing better than that to tell us? You, a class-leader and local preacher, what do you tell the people when you preach to them, if that is your experience?   You are like a man down in a dark cellar, with the shutters closed, in doleful gloom while the sun is shining outside. Take the shutters down, man, and let the light of heaven into your soul!'   At this point the leader interjected some remark, when Mr. Collins again interrupted him: 'Why, you are poking at the sink-hole, now; do take the shutters down, and let heaven and joy come into your soul.'   When Mr. Collins turned to the other leader for his experience he answered in much the same dull and melancholy tone.   When he had finished Mr. Collins expostulated with him in similar terms: 'Lissaman! Lissaman! what do you mean?   What do you tell the people when you go to preach? Go and fetch the Bible from the pulpit and read such a chapter and verse.'   Though present I do not remember the passage, but I recall Mr. Collins' reply when the leader had read it: 'Lissaman, either your experience is wrong, or else God is a liar; I leave you to settle the question.'   This incident illustrates the searching fidelity with which Thomas Collins performed his pastoral duties when meeting the members, and indicates the type of experience which he taught to be the privilege of the Christian believer.

I commenced writing a diary soon after my conversion. In scanning its pages, which date back to 1843, I find that its chief feature is its record of the fluctuations of my spiritual experience. It also registers the sermons I heard in various places. Its entries contain the names of such well-known ministers as Revs. Samuel Coley, John Farrar, Thomas Jackson, J. D. Geden (who became my class-leader at Richmond), besides those of many obscure local preachers under whose ministry I received much benefit in the formative period of my Christian life. My diary records also the beginnings of definite service for Methodism in the way of Sabbath School work, preaching, systematic tract distribution and cottage meetings. That my work was not invariably easy is clear from such records as the following : ' I met with some persecution while distributing tracts, but it only served to imbue me with fresh courage and strength.'

My eager efforts to improve my mental equipment are tabled in a passage from my diary, written at the age of eighteen, with which I will close this chapter :

'*May* 11, 1849.—I have been trying for some time past to improve my mind and cultivate with increased exertion my mental faculties. During the last eight or ten months I have acquired a tolerable knowledge of the German language; have written a paragraph on "Giving," which appeared in the *Christian Miscellany* for April; have written since then a few lines on the death of the Rev. A. E. Farrar, and a few lines of blank verse on "The Bible" to be inserted in the same periodical. Commenced this day to write a prize essay on the Moral, Social, and Intellectual Condition of the Working Classes, with a Remedy for Existing Evils. I find writing a good means of mental improvement. While improving the mind I would not forget the improvement of the soul, and let that become a wild and barren waste. That is awfully possible. Spiritual growth does not always keep pace with mental improvement. Constant prayer, especially private, with regular study of the Word of God, and diligent watchfulness are essential to maintain vigorous and healthy soul life. Lord, give me the constant power to pray!'

CHAPTER IV

FACING THE WORLD

'The wide world is all before us.'—Burns.

As already stated, the hope of completing my education at Coventry Grammar School was abandoned owing to the prohibitive fees. I was therefore reluctantly compelled, at the tender age of twelve, to turn out into the world to earn my living. As no better opening presented itself I had to begin as a baker's boy in the ancient city of Coventry. My occupation was neither easy nor pleasant, for my work commenced at 3 a.m. and continued until 9 p.m., and on Saturdays until midnight. It fell to my lot to heat the oven, make the dough, and bake the cakes. To have them ready for breakfast this early work was necessary, and to get them into the consumers' hands I had to traverse the streets with a fairly heavy load, crying 'Hot cakes and rolls' until my stock was disposed of. These duties being finished the rest of the day was filled up in baking bread and distributing it amongst shopkeepers and private customers. No wonder that with such exhausting work I was completely spent by bed-time; and on Sundays when at chapel I would often stand up during the sermon to keep myself awake. Some folk are apt to sigh that the former days were better than these. In some things that may be true; but it certainly does not apply to the hours of labour, and the opportunities for needed rest and recreation. The working classes never had better times than now. There may still be room for improvement in some directions, but social reform and humanitarian legislation have already done much to improve their condition.

I endured the severity of my lot for about twelve months, and then one Sunday morning, rising early, I wished my employer, with whom I lived, good-bye, and walked home, a distance of six miles, to my mother. My experience of the bakery business had been more than sufficient, and I could not be persuaded to return. Some new vocation had to be found for me, a difficult task for people cut off from the world in a remote hamlet that presented little opportunities of employment beyond agricultural labour.

My eldest brother was then carrying on the trade of a village shoemaker—which seems to have been the recognized family occupation, as all my brothers and some of our ancestors followed it. There being no other opening, I was engaged to this brother to learn the cord-wainer's art and craft. Believing that my steps were being ordered by the Lord, in answer to

MY MOTHER

my prayer, I tried to do my duty and make the best of the situation; but I never felt in my element. My work was very exacting; I had to be at the bench early and late, and found but scanty opportunity for reading and the culture of my mind. I felt shut out of all society, with no scope for advancement, and I longed to change my lot. Having no influential friends to lend a helping hand I was doomed to toil on, making and mending boots and shoes for three weary years. The only help available to obtain release from intolerable bondage was a sister engaged in domestic service in a Quaker family at Leicester. I entreated her assistance, and at her request her master interested himself in my case. Her employer's son-in-law was at that time vice-chairman of the Midland Railway, and his good offices were enlisted on my behalf.

I received a message through my sister that he had secured a situation for me at a railway station. What it was, or where it was, I was not informed. This mattered little to me, for I concluded that it might be better, but could scarcely be worse, than the distasteful occupation I was then following. I was directed to prepare myself to enter upon my work at once, and go to the vice-chairman at Leicester. He received me very kindly, took me to the station, kept the train waiting till he had given me full instructions, and then told the guard to stop the train—which was not scheduled to stop—and put me down at Staveley in Derbyshire.

All this was new and strange to me, for I had never travelled so far from home before. Though appreciated by one of a romantic turn of mind, there were some things in the changes taking place which made me sad. To say good-bye to my parents, especially my mother, and go to a place which I had never heard of, was trying to a youth strongly attached to home and family. On leaving, my mother put into my hand a piece of plum cake. I began to eat it, but when I turned and gave a last look at my childhood's home the cake seemed as though it would choke me, and I could not take another mouthful. I put what was left aside, and, without intending it at the time, I have carefully preserved it all through my life, for sixty-two years, and it is now regarded as a precious relic by my family.

Arriving at Staveley, I was spell-bound at the sight of an iron furnace, close to the railway. I had never seen anything like it before, and the furnace being of the old-fashioned type, with the blast roaring and belching forth flames out of the cupola, lighting up a sheet of water close by, and giving a lurid appearance to everything around, it seemed to my startled mind very much like the mouth of hell itself. Then came my interview with the station-master, a somewhat gruff and harsh type of humanity, who told me that he and I would have to do all the work. Of course it fell to *my* lot to undertake all the rough duties, while he performed the smooth. My work was to light the office fire, sweep the floor, work the signals when sufficiently initiated, clean and light the near and distant lamps, call out 'Staveley' as each train arrived, and carry the passengers' luggage to and from the trains. Various jobs, not properly mine, were imposed upon me, such as cleaning the station-master's boots, carrying water and other things for the service of the adjoining house where he lived.

All this was rather different from my dream, but I resolved to do my duty and adapt myself to the circumstances in which Providence had placed me. My greatest trial came when the station-master informed me that I must be on duty early next morning, which was Sunday, and that my work would continue on and off during the day. I had always cherished a feeling of sanctity about the Sabbath, and hitherto had enjoyed the privilege of spending it in worship and work for God. This was therefore a great blow to me, and I never became reconciled to it. I had no idea where my home would be, but learning where the late porter had lodged I went to ascertain if they could take me in. They consented to do so, and at once I removed my belongings to a plain-looking cottage in a long terrace occupied chiefly by colliers and foundry workers. It was very near to the station, but my duties were so incessant that frequently I could not leave my post, but had to eat my meals in public in the booking-office, then used by passengers as the only waiting-room.

c

I did not find much comfort in my new home, which contained a family of dirty little children, whose yells under the Saturday night tub were disagreeable in the extreme. After I had retired to my humble bed the husband came home in a state of intoxication, and a feud arose between himself and his wife which was painfully novel in my experience. My pillow that night was wet with bitter tears, and I longed to be back at home. I soon found more agreeable lodgings with Father Deakin, a good old Methodist, who loved his Bible and walked in the fear of the Lord. Mrs. Deakin was a clean and motherly woman, and the pair did all they could to make me happy and comfortable.

There were several earnest Methodists living in the same terrace, and it was their custom to hold frequent prayer-meetings, getting access to each cottage and taking them in turn for these gatherings. These men, most of whom were colliers, knew the secret of prevailing prayer. In their flannels, with bare chests, they called upon God in stentorian tones which could be heard for a considerable distance. 'The kingdom of heaven suffereth violence,' and the cottages were often crowded, while their simple but powerful wrestling brought Heaven's blessing down. There were glad and fervent responses from those who were of the Household of Faith, and now and again the cry of the penitent almost drowned the voice of the suppliant. At the first opportunity I repaired to the chapel in the village and made the acquaintance of the people, especially of two young men with whom I chummed and worked in God's cause.

In those days Mesmerism was being brought prominently before the public, and one of my two friends was an easy subject for treatment. I had never seen any one in a mesmeric state, but he consented for me to try my skill upon him. In a short time he was completely under my spell, and according as I exercised my will on him he nursed me on his knee, or prayed, or sang with startling effect. He had an exceptionally fine voice, and while in the mesmeric trance he sang in a way and to a tune I shall never forget—

> ' I'll praise my Maker while I've breath ;
> And when my voice is lost in death,
>   Praise shall employ my nobler powers :
> My days of praise shall ne'er be past,
> While life, or thought, or being last,
>   Or immortality endures.'

In singing the second line his voice faltered and became feebler, as if he were really dying. Having finished the séance I endeavoured to restore the normal condition by what I understood to be the usual method. For a time there was no response, and I began to get alarmed, until my repeated efforts at last proved successful.

I had a great desire to be mesmerized myself, and a friend, away in the village, undertook to operate upon me. The good old-fashioned folk with whom I lodged were greatly concerned about this. They regarded mesmerism as a black

C 2

art, a machination of the devil, and used their utmost efforts to dissuade me from what they declared to be a wicked thing. Being rashly determined to try the experiment, I kept my appointment at the house of my friend, a mile distant. The attempt to put me under hypnotic influence failed, though prolonged till midnight, and I returned alone at that witching hour to my lodgings. As I made my way back in the dead of night, along lonely footpaths and through pitch-black fields, my conscience began to tell me that perhaps the old people were right. With an inflamed imagination and an uneasy conscience I reached a spot where it was rumoured a ghost had been seen. Just as I climbed a stile and turned my eye towards the eerie spot, to my horror there was the veritable spectre in the form of flickering tongues of flame. For the moment I was riveted to the ground, with my hair seeming to stand on end, and my eye involuntarily held by the grim phantom before me. After a brief interval I regained a little courage and began to move, at first stealthily, then faster and faster, until I furiously dashed along, leaping over stiles, and at length reached my destination, dropping down speechless and exhausted into a vacant chair.

The old man, feeling sure that some disaster would follow my wrong action, had sat up long past his usual time for retiring, and was anxiously waiting the return of the recreant prodigal. Seeing the excited state I was in, he asked what was the matter. As I had not sufficient breath to answer he inquired again more anxiously, 'Whatever is the matter?' As soon as I recovered speech I blurted out, 'I've seen——!' but was unable to finish the sentence. When I had further recovered I exclaimed, 'I've seen—I've seen a ghost!' Presently I was composed enough to give a more detailed account of the incident, which so impressed the old man that he rose very early next morning, before going to work down the pit, to visit the haunted spot and track the ghost.

On returning from the investigation he made me the object of a considerable amount of chaff. 'Ha! ye soft,' he exclaimed, 'what do ye think it was that frightened ye so?' 'It was certainly a ghost,' I replied. 'Yes,' he retorted, 'a fine ghost it was; it was in a plough-field where they had been gathering twitch (couch-grass) during the day and had left a heap burning under the hedgerow. When you saw it, it happened to be blazing up and appeared like a ghost.' But for that disillusionment I should certainly have maintained to the end that I had encountered a veritable ghost. How many ghostly apparitions might be similarly explained away if only we knew the stuff of which they are made!

I remained at Staveley from July 1847 till May 1848, when I was seized with small-pox and was invalided home to be nursed. Before that date, however, I had resolved to seek another change where I could find more congenial employment and have my Sundays free. With this end in view I put an advertisement in the *Methodist Magazine*, and while convalescent and still at home I received a reply which led to a remarkable change and opened a new epoch in my life, as recorded in the next chapter.

CHAPTER V

MOVING UPWARD

'Progress is the law of life.'—*Browning*.

MY advertisement in the *Methodist Magazine* brought a letter from Dr. Ellis, proprietor of the Hydropathic Establishment at Sudbrook Park, Richmond, Surrey. The writer requested me to meet him at Piccadilly at twelve o'clock on the following day. The summons reached me in my native village. Very few, if any, persons living in that rural neighbourhood had ever been to London. Some of my friends, concluding it was a hoax, tried to persuade me not to go; but I was too anxious to get away from my distasteful occupation to heed any counter advice. The news rapidly spread that I had received a call to London, and I became quite a hero in consequence. Some of the neighbours wished me 'Good-bye,' assured I should never return from my wild adventure. Making my way to Coventry, the nearest station on the main line to London, I took train for Euston, whence I proceeded to Piccadilly, which I reached at the appointed hour.

An uncouth lad, green from the country, with the scars of small-pox still visible on my face—the wonder is that Dr. Ellis did not summarily dismiss me as altogether unsuitable for the important post of secretary and cashier in his establishment. On the contrary, he received me courteously, and treated me with extreme consideration and kindness, gave me some particulars of the duties required, and asked if I thought I could discharge them satisfactorily.

Seeing at once that the hour of my opportunity had arrived, yet feeling at the same time my total unfitness for such an appointment, after hesitating for a moment I said, ' If you will have patience and bear with me for a time I will undertake to do the work to your satisfaction.' He concluded the interview with the words, ' I am afraid you will not do ; but I will think it over and write you in a few days.' Putting £2 into my hand to defray my expenses he wished me good-bye, and I returned home.

The journey, which can now be done in less than two hours, at that time filled up nearly the whole day; for the parliamentary train, in which I travelled, stopped at every station, and waited at Blisworth at least an hour for the passengers to get refreshment. My friends were glad, but not a little surprised, to see me back again, especially so soon.

After a week's anxious suspense the promised letter at length arrived, and to my intense delight it announced that the situation was open for my acceptance, and requested me to prepare to enter upon its duties without delay. I promptly placed my slender possessions in a plain elm box, and hied away with a feeling of glee. Arriving at Euston I hailed a cabman to drive me to Sudbrook Park, thinking it was some place within a short radius, and never dreaming that it was twelve or fourteen miles distant. The cabby discreetly kept his counsel, merely telling me to 'Jump up!' Mile after mile we pursued our seemingly interminable way; but every journey has its end, and at length the driver stopped at the lodge entrance of a beautifully timbered park. My fear that some mistake had been made was relieved on inquiries made of the lodge-keeper. Driving down a winding carriage-road, I was brought up in front of a stately mansion situated in the midst of the park. A porter in livery answered my timid ringing of the bell at the conservatory entrance, and, learning my name, said, 'It's all right; come in.' I had now to settle with the cabman, which nearly emptied my purse. My wages as a railway servant having been only twelve shillings per week my savings were exceedingly small. The porter conducted me to a comfortable sitting-room, reserved for the exclusive use of myself and the steward, who had charge of the farm, park, and gardens.

In due course I was introduced to Mrs. Ellis and an only daughter, a child of tender age. I seemed all at once to have got into a new world, with an environment so entirely different from all I had been accustomed to. Sudbrook was once a ducal residence. Subsequently converted into a hydropathic establishment, it was first opened as such by Priessnitz himself, the originator of the Water Cure. The house was commodious and beautiful, and found employment for a staff of twenty or thirty servants of various grades. The diningroom, one of the finest and most spacious I have ever seen, was decorated with exquisite oak carvings by Grinling Gibbons, and contained a sculptured marble mantelpiece said to have cost £2,000. I mention these things that the reader may the better understand the strangeness and wonderment of my feelings in being suddenly transferred from the hard lot of a wayside railway porter to such luxurious surroundings.

Sudbrook Park consisted of about 100 acres of land, and adjoined Richmond Park with its palatial residences of noblemen of high rank. Our nearest neighbour was Lord John Russell, whose delightfully situated mansion commanded extensive views overlooking the Thames. From Richmond Hill might be seen one of the finest views in England, overlooking a lovely landscape whose sweep took in Windsor Castle. It was here that Thomson wrote his poem on 'The Seasons,' the spot being marked by a board, bearing an extract from the poem, affixed to a tree. In the immediate neighbourhood was Petersham, where King Charles I once lived, and from whence he made his escape

SUDBROOK PARK, 1850

before his execution. His palace abutted on the river, on which he spent his leisure hours in his 'happy days,' as represented in the familiar picture.

The Wesleyan Theological College was near by, and within its classic shades were students who were destined to eminence in the ministry of the Methodist Church. It was about this time that Charles Garrett, Samuel Coley, W. O. Simpson and others, whose names afterwards became household words, were in training. The college staff consisted of Samuel Jackson, the Governor; Thomas Jackson, Theological Tutor; John Farrar, Classical Tutor; with John Dury Geden as Assistant Tutor. Not one of these, and very few of the students of those days, are living.

I was taken to my office by Dr. Ellis, and was told that I should have to do the correspondence, keep the books, receive and disburse the cash, engage the servants and pay their wages, with sundry other functions connected with my post. The work was a great contrast to my late employment, but Dr. Ellis took considerable pains in helping me to understand and master my duties. I have always felt the deepest gratitude to him for a training which was more educational than all the schooling I had received. His influence in the development of my character was incalculable. I recall how on one occasion when he directed me to do something I answered that I could not, it was impossible. He gave me a look which pierced me through, and said, '"Impossible"?

Never use that word again, sir!' Then eyeing me from head to foot he added, 'You can move the world if you like.'

When I had become accustomed to my new sphere, and was polished up a bit, in the absence of the chief it fell to my lot to take his place at the head of the table, and preside over visitors and patients—such as Sir Francis-Burdett, his daughter (who became Baroness Burdett-Coutts), and other people of similar rank. This was rather a large order for an erstwhile railway porter. My story requires that I should say that Dr. Ellis, though so extremely kind, had the one failing of a violent temper, and when I had been in his service some little time he would mark his dissatisfaction with my performance of any duty by saying, 'I think you had better take notice and leave.' At length I took him at his word: 'All right, sir; then I go this day month.' Soon after my departure he sent for me again, and I willingly returned. This was repeated several times, until I left finally in November 1851, being desirous of taking another step up the ladder.

On my departure the doctor presented me with a copy of his book on Hydropathy, *Hints to the Sick, the Lame, and the Lazy*, which I preserve and value because of the generous sentiments which are inscribed in his handwriting on its flyleaf: 'Mr. David Barr, with Dr. Ellis' best wishes and admiration of his excellent character and conduct during a long residence officially in his establishment at Sudbrook Park.—Nov. 1851.' Years later, when Dr. Ellis honoured me with a friendly visit, he confided in me in the following terms, which reveal the warm sympathy of his nature : 'I can speak to you now familiarly as a friend, and tell you that when I first saw you I knew you were not at all qualified for the situation I gave you, but I thought there was something in you that could be developed, and so with much pleasure I undertook the task.'

I had now to address myself to the work of finding some new vocation. Being desirous of seeing the country and acquiring experience in commercial life, I thought a berth as traveller for a business firm would afford me these facilities. A London gentleman of my acquaintance having taken out a patent for a sugar-chopping machine, I solicited a commission from him. He readily assented, providing me with a case in which to carry a sample machine. This I found a tiring undertaking, for the article itself weighed about 28 lbs. To make my burden feel heavier, for some time I travelled about from grocer to grocer, and from town to town, without taking a single order. This was so disappointing and different from my expectations that my patience almost reached breaking point and I was on the verge of despair. I soon plucked up heart, however, and chided myself for being such a coward. I went to my work again with new determination, and was at last rewarded in booking an order which I forwarded to my firm with great satisfaction. As time went on I succeeded better and better, and secured another commission from a Bradford manufacturer of soap-cutters, treacle taps, cans, &c. Business was prospering now, but I could not get my orders executed fast enough, and some were cancelled in consequence.

I was now making money fairly fast, and if there had been a reliable person at hand to execute all my orders and dispatch the goods with promptitude I should have done extremely well. My profits amounted to about £20 per week, so that I was saving money rather rapidly for a young man of twenty-one. With my savings I bought a piece of building land in my native village and began erecting four cottages, and 'thereby hangs a tale.' My old comrade, the steward at Sudbrook, informed me that very good cottages were constructed at his native place, Wellington in Somerset, with garden soil, and he offered to send a man to superintend my work; but the process of removing the soil within a wooden frame seemed to me so simple that I declined his offer. My building went on merrily till the walls were nearly high enough for the bedroom joists, when on going to inspect the work one morning, lo and behold the walls had fallen down and there lay before me a heap of ruins! Amidst the laughter and jeers of those who had prophesied failure I had the *débris* removed and began to build with bricks and mortar.

My expensive lessons in the school of experience

were not yet ended. When I had completed this unfortunate venture, and had saved a little more money, I took a small farm which proved to be a loss instead of a gain. The only satisfaction I obtained was in closing a public-house on the farm, which had led many astray, and which has never been opened since the day I closed it. In spite of the non-success of my first attempt at farming I was induced to try my hand again, but the result was far from encouraging.

I next engaged myself as commercial traveller to a nail and general hardware factor, with whom I continued until I again thought I could improve my position. With this end in view I made an engagement with a firm of merchants in Birmingham to travel on part salary and part commission. On the eve of starting on my first journey one of the principals proposed to alter the terms of agreement. Looking on this as dishonourable, and at once making up my mind that no good could result from representing such a firm, I wished him 'Good-day' and promptly left. Being now out of employment, so eager was I to get work that, after long and weary waiting, I offered my services to one firm for fifteen shillings per week, but without avail.

The variety of my experiences was not yet exhausted. After a service taken as supply for a local preacher in one of the Birmingham chapels, a member of the congregation came to me, and, ascertaining that I was without a situation, requested me to call upon him at his factory. This I did next morning, when he gave me a letter of introduction to a relative who was in the Insurance business. I gladly accepted a berth as canvasser and clerk, but could not get on to my satisfaction, either with my work or my master. My employer's brother, finding that I was not in my element, offered me a situation as clerk and collector in his business. He was a glass and lead merchant, and a local preacher, and I found things much more congenial and to my taste.

It was at this time that, through connecting myself with New Town Row Wesleyan Chapel, I formed the acquaintance of the late Mr. J. G. Newey's family. Mr. Newey was held in great respect in Methodist and other circles in Birmingham. The family had belonged to our Church since the days of John Wesley. Mr. Newey's father or grandfather appears to have entertained Mr. Wesley, and it is told that on one occasion when the latter was his guest, Mr. Newey, attired in a new suit of clothes, accompanied the great evangelist to the Bull Ring to preach. Both of them were pelted with rotten eggs. It was Sunday, and on returning, Mrs. Newey, perturbed at the bespattered condition of her husband's new suit, inquired of Mr. Wesley if it would be a desecration of the Sabbath to sponge and clean the soiled garments. The approval that was given satisfied her scruples. During the great agitation of '49 Mr. J. G. Newey had some exciting experiences when, as a Trustee, he maintained the rights of the 'Old Body' to property which the Reformers endeavoured forcibly to seize.

My acquaintance with the family grew into intimacy, and in the year 1854 I was privileged to lead Mr. Newey's second daughter to the bridal altar, where we began a truly happy life of marriage union. I was then receiving a salary which necessitated the exercise of most rigid economy, but my 'better self' was in full sympathy with my ambition to improve my position, and was ready to make sacrifices to accomplish this end. With her co-operation, and by strange good fortune, I was able to acquire a small property, so that we entered upon our married life in fulfilment of a previously-made resolution to live if possible in a house that belonged to us. My next speculation was in taking out a patent, with the profits of which, when disposed of, I obtained the equity of redemption of a small property. In this, however, I found I had been deliberately and cunningly deceived by the vendors, and was compelled to regard it as a bad investment. Thus I was still learning, and paying dearly for some of my lessons.

D

CHAPTER VI

STARTING BUSINESS

' Nothing is impossible to industry.'—Periander.

BEING by nature of a somewhat independent disposition, I had long made up my mind not to remain a hireling all my days, but to be my own master at the first opportunity that presented itself. I have recorded that I had already made tentative excursions in this direction which did not develop into permanent form. Without capital and with very little experience, I was conscious of the difficulties of starting business with assurance of success. I had to wait long, and keep an open eye on what was going on in the commercial world, before meeting with anything practical and within my means. There is a measure of fascination in laying the foundation of, and building up, a business, even with an occasional set-back. What I record here may encourage other young men who are struggling as I did, in the face of difficulties, to establish a business on their own account. This must be my excuse for stating how, step by step, my efforts were gradually rewarded with success.

While on the look-out for a suitable opening, I saw a notice of the death of a house and estate agent in Birmingham, and promptly took steps to ascertain if there was any chance of picking up some of the business, offering to the widow a fair price for anything I might thus secure. In this way I obtained the agency of a small property, which it is true brought in very little, but it was a beginning. My employer consented to my giving part of my time for a moiety of the salary I had been receiving, and moreover he put me in charge of a small block of house property which belonged to him. This was an arrangement of great advantage to me, and I now set to work in real earnest, resolved to give my best attention to any business, however trifling, that might come in my way. I distributed a large number of circulars, one of which dropped casually into a letter-box and secured me the collection of a whole street of houses. I also undertook the periodical collection of accounts for a manufacturer, making regular visits to London and Bristol. I believe I did this to his entire satisfaction, for on retiring from his business he employed me to find a purchaser for it, and authorized me to invest the proceeds in house property, leaving the matter entirely to my judgement and declining even to inspect most of it before purchasing. He entrusted me with the absolute management of the property, appointed me his

D 2

sole executor, and at his death I had the duty of realizing his estate and dividing the proceeds according to the terms of his will. I was encouraged to believe that I had given satisfaction in these transactions, as the family unanimously joined in making me a presentation in acknowledgement of my services.

In these ways my business grew until it demanded my whole attention, and I was compelled to relinquish entirely the work I had been doing for my employer. In a previous chapter I mentioned that I was furthered, to the point of sacrifice, by my wife, who entered heartily into my aims and endeavours. For a time my office was the sitting-room of the house where I lived; but business callers were now so numerous as to destroy the privacy of our home life and to necessitate making provision elsewhere. Anxious to keep down expenses—a very important rule for those who desire to make their way in life—instead of renting a suite of costly rooms, I bought the lease of a coach-house in the centre of the town, and converted the place into a waiting-room and office. When I had outgrown these premises I was able to dispose of them at a considerable profit. I next took a lease of some tumble-down property, which I rebuilt, occupying a portion for my business and letting off the remainder so as to leave me rent free and yield a good surplus income. By this time my business had happily been so successful that I had saved sufficient money to do a little in building and buying property. In such ways I gradually extended my connexion and accumulated capital. Perhaps my largest venture was in acquiring the option of purchase of an estate of 500 acres, with minerals underneath, at a cost of £32,000, paying down £1,000 as arranged. Others joined me in this venture, and within the specified time I was able to find a purchaser at £40,000. It will have been readily seen, however, by readers of this narrative that my judgement was not infallible. I had to encounter occasional losses; but of these I need not speak further, for on the whole God has greatly prospered my business life.

Apart from matters of profit and loss, like other commercial men I have had a share of disagreeable experiences in my business career. Let me tell one sorrowful story, which I record as an admonitory example. I took into my service as clerk a young man who was a local preacher, and who for several years proved a faithful employé and gave me every satisfaction. To my great surprise I eventually discovered that he had been extensively robbing me. I called him into my office, and he admitted the delinquency. Falling on his knees he frankly confessed everything and craved forgiveness. I said to him, ' Tell me what has led you astray. I know you were once an honest man and a good Christian; whatever has been the cause of your ruin?' He said in reply, 'I made the acquaintance of a young man who was formerly a fellow clerk of yours. My sole purpose was to do him good and get him converted ; but he has been my ruin. No sooner had I formed his acquaintance than he said to me, " Come and have a glass with me." I resisted the temptation at first, but at last yielded, and went with him to a public-house. He asked me again and again, and I went each time with less pressure than before. At last I got into the habit of spending my evenings at the public-house instead of going home to my wife and children. The thirst for drink grew upon me and became so strong that I began to take your money to satisfy it when I had spent all my own, and I am now a ruined man as the result.' His broken-hearted wife came to me and with sobs and tears said, ' Oh, I never thought it would come to this—that my husband, once a kind and good Christian man, would so disgrace himself and his family. I would rather have put him into his coffin and followed him to the grave, struggling on as best I could with my fatherless children. Oh! what shall I do?' Such is often the end of the first step in the downward path. How all-important it is to guard against the earliest temptation !

My connexion with the business concern which I had created continued until 1879, when, owing to a failure in my health, I retired, disposing of my interest to my partner, formerly my clerk, whose fidelity had led me to take him in as co-principal some time previous. This was not, as I anticipated, to be the end of my commercial career. Years later I joined my son in giving him a start in business; and after remaining until we had built up an extensive and valuable connexion, I retired at the mature age of seventy-eight, having, as I think, earned repose from the anxieties and responsibilities of business life.

CHAPTER VII

PUBLIC LIFE

' I am a citizen of the world.'—Diogenes Laertius.

I HAVE long entertained the opinion that what is known as public life should not be left entirely to men of the world, but that Christians should be ready to take their part as they have the opportunity. The danger is lest, when they respond to the call and are elected to public offices, they should be drawn in too far and give time and attention which should be devoted to business, family claims, and Church work. Many have been led astray and have become so engrossed that they have been seriously injured in body and soul, and in some cases it has ended in complete ruin. Openings for public work readily multiply to willing and capable men, and it is most essential that they be on their guard lest they are drawn into the vortex.

My first call to public service occurred in 1866, when I was elected a member of the Board of Lighting Inspectors, the only local governing authority of the suburb where I resided. In those days watchmen, as they were called, patrolled the thoroughfares of the district, calling out each hour of the night, and sometimes the state of the weather, in stentorian tones. Three years later a Board of Health was formed, of which I was one of the first elected members. I continued on the Board until 1877, being twice elected to fill the office of Chairman.

On the passing of the 1870 Education Act I was invited by the Liberal Party to become one of their candidates for the new School Board. Though not a pronounced political partisan, my vote was generally cast on the Liberal side ; hence the overture from that quarter on this occasion. I was compelled, however, to join issue with the party on the question of Bible teaching, their programme being that of secular education. The other side then asked me to join them, to which I consented on the understanding that my connexion with them was on no other ground than that of Bible teaching, and that I should not be expected to subscribe to their entire programme. I was duly returned, but the advocates of religious teaching were in a minority for six years, during which time angry and sometimes fierce debates took place between the contending parties. At the election of 1876 the party with which I was associated secured a majority on the Board, and from that time until the present Bible instruction has had a recognized place in the curriculum.

For a short time I was called to serve the community as a Guardian of the Poor in the suburban district in which I lived; and for six years I had a seat on the Birmingham Board of Guardians, and took an active part in the onerous duties connected with that position. I felt great interest in this work, although a guardian is often brought into contact with sights and has to listen to stories that are sad and painful in the extreme.

Owing to the position I conscientiously took up at the School Board election I was blackballed by the Liberal Party. They called me a turn-coat, denounced me as a renegade, and threatened to have their revenge. Their opportunity came at the next election for the Local Board of Health, when they succeeded in defeating my return at the polls. Not content with this, when as Vice-Chairman of the Birmingham Board of Guardians I should have been promoted to the Chair, their efforts were again successful in securing my rejection. When they had completed their work I turned to some of the leaders of the Party and said, 'I thank you very much, gentlemen; you have done me a great kindness—unwittingly it may be, but it is none the less true. I have given a large share of my time and energy to public work; I have injured my health and neglected important duties; but you have now set me free, and I thank you for your kindness.' They endeavoured to oust me from the School Board also, but this attempt failed. I remained a member for fifteen years, until, on my removal to another part of the town, I voluntarily retired.

For some time I was a member of the Rural Labourers' League, of which the Right Hon. Jesse Collings was chairman—an association formed to assist working men in towns and villages to get a plot of land on easy terms for their occupation and benefit.

I may mention in this connexion that in 1864 I was elected a Director of the Wesleyan and General Assurance Society, a Trustee in 1875, and Vice-Chairman in 1901. The Society has had a unique and interesting history. About the year 1841 a few leading Wesleyans, including my wife's father who was one of the founders and the first member, met in the vestry of Cherry Street Chapel to consider what could be done to keep young men who were members of the Church from public-house sick-clubs, which proved in so many cases to be a source of moral peril. They resolved to start a friendly society under the name of 'The Wesleyan Provident Society,' to provide a weekly allowance in sickness and a certain amount at death. The name of the organization was subsequently altered to 'The Wesleyan and General Assurance Society,' in order to admit into membership those of the general public who desired to join. Later, a special Act of Parliament was obtained to widen the scope of its operations. From such humble beginnings it has now risen to a position which may fairly entitle it to be ranked amongst the foremost Industrial Life Offices of the day, enrolling in membership considerably more than a quarter of a million of policy-holders. It is interesting to note that although it has long since ceased to have any organic connexion with the Church in which it was born, it is still obligatory that three-fourths of its directors shall be members of the Wesleyan Church, and the Board meetings are always opened with prayer.

CHAPTER VIII

CHURCH WORK

'To look up and not down,
To look forward and not back,
To look out and not in—and
To lend a hand.'—*Hale*.

As soon as I experienced the converting grace of God I felt a longing desire that others should be made happy like myself. Very few doors were open for service, to a lad not yet twelve years of age, in connexion with a small cause in a scattered hamlet, but a holy compulsion was upon me to attempt something, however trifling. Even at that immature age I began to take a class in the village Sunday school, comprising only a very few scholars. Tract distribution, personal invitations from house to house to the services of the chapel, and the collection of moneys for Methodist periodicals, afforded additional spheres of usefulness. As time went on, a desire to preach the gospel—which I interpreted as a call from God—stole upon me. My thoughts often turned in that direction long before a call came from the Church. When still very young, I remember climbing to the top of an apple-tree in my father's orchard to prepare my first sermon. I had no difficulty—as mature preachers sometimes have—in selecting a text, for my mind soon settled upon the familiar passage from Jeremiah, 'The harvest is past, the summer is ended, and we are not saved.' My difficulty began as soon as I had written down the text, when I came to a dead stand, and felt like the local preacher who was compelled to say, 'There are many profound and beautiful thoughts in this passage, but they do not occur to me just now.'

Towards the end of my twentieth year, the Rev. Charles Janion, superintendent of the Coventry Circuit, after serious conversation with me, put me on the Plan as a local preacher on trial. My first sermon was preached in a house at Corley Ash from the text, 'The sufferings of Christ and the glory that should follow' (1 Pet. i. 11). In after years I ceased to preach on the subject, feeling it was too profound; but a rash beginner will sometimes boldly enter in where angels might fear to tread. I see from my diary that I had a good time: it does not follow that my hearers shared my experience !

After the usual term of probation I presented myself for what I felt to be the terrible ordeal of examination before the Local Preachers' Quarterly Meeting. As with many another in like circumstances, nervousness almost paralysed my power of thought and utterance. In answer to the question whether we are saved by faith or by works, I re-

FILLONGLEY WESLEYAN CHURCH, 1893

(See p. 111)

plied, 'By works'; and when asked for Scripture proof, I quoted a passage which proved the contrary: 'By grace are ye saved through faith, and that not of yourselves; it is the gift of God; not of works, lest any man should boast.' Notwithstanding this serious blunder, the Meeting conferred upon me the position of a fully accredited local preacher.

Removing to Birmingham in 1854, I was directed to lodgings near New Town Row Chapel, and my name was placed on the local preachers' Plan of the Belmont Row Circuit. I frequently accompanied the open-air Band, but shrank from out-door speaking, until I was ashamed of myself and felt condemned for my cowardice. The noble example of Dr. Miller, then Vicar of Birmingham parish church, led me to make the attempt. I soon discovered that God had blessed me with a suitable voice for such work, and I resolved that henceforth it should be consecrated to His service. Ere long all shyness and reluctance left me, and I have from that time till now felt great delight in the work. I remember on one occasion taking part in an open-air service near New Town Row Chapel, when one of our Band, a great, brawny, and plain-spoken but zealous Christian, had his righteous anger roused by the disturbance of a number of low-bred and shabbily-garbed slaves of Satan. He stood the interruption as long as he could, and then drawing up to the scoffers, eyeing them from head to foot, and taking good stock of their appearance, said in his broad dialect and strong voice, 'If I was the devil I should be asheamed o' me men!' This crushing sally was like a bolt from the blue, and instantly produced the desired result.

In 1876 I removed from Aston Manor to Hagley Road in the Islington Circuit, where I continued to take an active part in Church work. I joined the prayer-leaders' Band, engaging in cottage services, preaching in turn at a common lodging-house, in large courts, and in other places. After speaking on one such occasion I was interested to learn that a person who lived in an adjoining court overheard some remarks made in the course of my address which led to his conversion; and I am grateful to have reason for believing that these humble efforts were made a blessing to others. Such work is not without its humorous incidents. In connexion with a great Evangelistic Mission at Islington Chapel, our Band paraded the neighbouring streets early one Sunday morning, singing and exhorting the people to attend the services. The Rev. Joseph Posnett, superintendent of the circuit, was with us. As he was speaking some of the folk appeared at their bedroom windows in their night attire to see what was going on. Mr. Posnett in his hearty way urged them to accept an invitation to the services, adding, 'Come, just as you are!' in blissful unconsciousness of the comic humour of the situation.

Since coming to Islington circuit I have had the honour of filling the offices of Poor steward, Society steward, and Circuit steward, besides holding various secretaryships and treasurerships, not to mention service on Connexional Committees. It has been my privilege to attend many District Synods, and I have been seven times elected a representative to Conference. I believe I have filled every office in Methodism open to a layman, except that of class-leader. I have repeatedly declined this post, feeling that I could not do justice to such a work without interfering with other duties; but I have always counted it a privilege to attend the class-meeting as regularly as possible.

My interest in the Local Preachers' Mutual Aid Association was deeply aroused in 1890 at a great public meeting in Carrs Lane Chapel in connexion with the Aggregate Meeting of the Association. Since then I have done what I could to forward its interests. I was elected a member of the General Committee, and have never failed to attend the Aggregate Meeting. It has been a great joy to go up and down the country advocating from pulpit and platform, to the best of my ability, the claims of sick and aged brethren who have rendered invaluable service to village Methodism, and of the widows of deceased brethren in straitened circumstances. At the York Aggregate Meeting in 1905 I was chosen President-elect of the Association, and accordingly was called to the Chair at the Aggregate Meeting in Bradford the following June. In the interval I was laid aside by serious illness, and my doctor prohibited my

E

undertaking the heavy duties of my prospective office. His objection was sustained by many friends, and I was plunged into great perplexity as to what my duty was. In my morning reading just at that time, my attention was arrested by Isa. xii. 10, 'Fear thou not, for I am with thee; be not dismayed, for I am thy God; I will strengthen thee, yea I will help thee, yea I will uphold thee with the right hand of My righteousness.' These words came with great power as a message direct from Heaven. They settled the question, and my mind was now quite made up to go trusting in the strength of the Lord. The result justified my decision, for strength was given according to my need. I travelled about 8,400 miles during the year, preached twice nearly every Sunday, addressed many public meetings, and attended almost every meeting of the Committee. On no occasion had I to seek a supply for my pulpit appointments, and I finished the year physically better than at the beginning. The incessant work brought great enjoyment, and proved to be a means of grace. The crowning honour in connexion with my public engagements was conferred when I was appointed to occupy Wesley's pulpit in the Cathedral of Methodism.

I will close this chapter by repeating what I said in an earlier one, that I have found more recreation and pleasure in Christian and philanthropic work than in any worldly amusement. Some years ago a client, a young man, left an orphan and heir to considerable wealth, called at my office. In course of conversation he inquired, 'Do you ever go to the theatre?' 'No,' I replied, 'I have not come down to that yet.' 'Why, I should be at a great loss for recreation,' he remarked, 'if I could not go to the theatre.' I answered, 'You are a much younger man than I am, and I may venture to offer a little advice. When you feel in need of recreation let me advise you to find your way to one of the back streets or alleys of Birmingham ; go into the house of some poverty-stricken family; take a bit of sunshine with you, and some of the money God has bestowed upon you so plentifully.' When I had finished, he said, 'Yes, it is all very good, but not in my way.' Then taking a handful of silver from his pocket he told me to use it in his stead. I replied, 'I wanted you to do it for the pleasure you would get out of it ; but if you will not, I shall be quite willing to be your almoner.' He returned some time afterwards, when I said to him, 'If you had seen the look of surprise and gladness on the face of that poor woman sitting on a stone step in Temple Row, with her crutches by her side, and a sickly-looking baby on her lap, when I put some of your silver into her hand, you would have derived more pleasure than is to be got out of the theatre.' My report so far gratified him that he gave me a fresh supply of cash for further charitable work on his behalf.

E 2

CHAPTER IX

EVANGELISTIC WORK

'Men die in darkness at your side
Without a hope to cheer the tomb.'—*Bonar.*

MY story would not be complete if I did not
devote some space to an account of my experiences
in a type of Christian service which has always
commanded my special sympathy and in which
for a time I was able to take an active interest.
Soon after my conversion I had a great desire, if
Providence should prepare the way, to spend the
latter part of my life in conducting Evangelistic
Missions with the view of helping the cause of God
in rural places. Being myself a product of village
Methodism, I felt I was specially indebted thereto.
Many of the most stalwart sons of our Church
in urban circuits emanate from obscure country
places, and it is to me a source of profound regret
that in so large a number of villages the cause
has languished and in some has ceased to exist.
To spend time and energy in assisting village
Methodism seemed to me a call from God, and the
conviction became so strong that I laid my plans
to acquire a sufficient competence to enable me to

consecrate at least a portion of my time in gratuitous service to that branch of work. At last I thought I had reached a point when I could afford to render help of this sort in places where it would be acceptable and might be useful. I was in dead earnest, and after consulting the Rev. Samuel Coley and discussing with him every aspect of the question, I was strongly counselled by him to obey what appeared to be a divine call. At the invitation of Mr. Coley, who in the interval had removed from Birmingham to the Highbury Circuit, I commenced revival services at Queen's Road Mission Hall on January 23, 1871. I went in fear and trembling, but was greatly helped and encouraged in seeing many brought to a knowledge of the truth.

In such work one sees the seamy side of human life, and meets with many sad and disappointing cases. Accompanied by the lay Missioner, I visited a thieves' den. I asked one of the men if he had started for heaven, and received the prompt and candid reply, 'No, I haven't! There's no mistake about that! I've lived a very middling sort of life. I'd been doing something wrong once, and a policeman caught me. Instead of treating me like a gentleman he began in a rough sort of way. It stirred the devil in me, and it took sixteen men to get me to the lock-up.' In another house which I visited were a man and wife and several little children living and sleeping in one wretched room. I learnt that the man was once in affluent circumstances, and had kept his carriage, but was now so reduced that they were without food, and had been fasting for some time. On another occasion, in going round to speak to those who remained at one of the after-meetings, I addressed a woman with ragged clothing and dishevelled hair and the stamp of vice and misery on her face. When I inquired if she were on her way to heaven, she fiercely retorted, 'What is that to you? You are a Judas Iscariot! So help me God, you are!' The Missioner called to her from the other end of the room, 'Hush! don't insult Mr. Barr; he has come all the way from Birmingham to try to do you good.' 'I don't care if he has come from hell!' she responded. She came again the following evening, and seemed in quite a different mood. Shaking her by the hand I said, 'Now I know the good Spirit of God is striving with you, and if you will give up the drink I shall have some hope of you.' 'Stop that!' she cried, for I had touched the quick. Before the meeting closed she seemed very penitent, but was so bound by the fetters of sin and vice that she did not find deliverance, and never came again. I ascertained that she had been brought up respectably in a minister's family, and had fallen to the low level in which I saw her through strong drink. These are but samples of the disappointments a Missioner has to encounter in evangelistic work.

During my stay I met with many incidents of a very different nature which much cheered me in my work. I was taken, in visiting, to a good old

Christian who was bedridden and dependent on charity. He lay on a poor pallet in an attic, afflicted and in deep poverty, but was as happy as a king—far happier than many a one who wears a crown. During our conversation I observed, 'You have lost the sight of one of your eyes?' 'Yes,' he said, ' my heavenly Father has taken it, and He shall have the other if He likes.' In leaving I wished him good-bye, adding, ' We may never meet again on earth, but by God's grace we will meet in heaven.' 'Yes,' he replied with a bright smile on his face, ' I'm climbing up the ladder, and am near the top ; I shall soon be there ! '

The two servants of my host were seized with deep conviction of sin at the Sunday evening service. In the after-meeting they were in great distress, and went home unhappy. Their tears and sobs at family worship were distressing. They retired to their rooms, but not to sleep ; they spent a good part of the night in weeping and prayer, and continued in the same state till I left London. I was sorry to go away leaving them burdened with the guilt of sin, but I had explained the way of salvation in the simplest way I could ; I had prayed with them and for them, and was unable to help them further. On the day after my return I received a letter from my host with the following welcome news : 'You will be glad to hear at the earliest moment that our elder servant found the Lord directly after you left. When I returned to business after bidding you farewell at the railway-station my little son came in haste and said I must go home at once, as one of the servants was in great distress. When I got there I found her in an ecstasy of joy. When she had calmed a little I asked her how the Lord had revealed Himself so blessedly to her soul. "Oh!" she said, "directly after Mr. Barr left I felt that I was a lost soul, and that there was no hope for me. Just at that moment I thought of my erring husband; he has been a very wicked and cruel man to me, but I felt I could forgive him, and I asked God to forgive him too. Instantly light and peace came into my soul, and I rose from my knees happy in God." No doubt,' my friend added, 'that feeling of bitterness and enmity towards her husband had kept her so long without the blessing.'

I find that from 1871, for about ten years, on and off, I held missions at such places as Brailsford in the Ashford Circuit, Bilston, Barwell in the Hinckley Circuit, Uttoxeter, Earl Shilton, Littleport in the Ely Circuit, Ashbourne, Wirksworth, Greenwich, Kidderminster, Redditch, Whitchurch, Droitwich, Barton-on-Humber, Old Park in Shropshire, New Holland, Gateshead, Bloxwich, Bloomsbury Mission Hall in Birmingham, Willenhall, Kington, and Burlawn in Cornwall. Several of these places I visited for a second, and in some cases for a third mission. The gracious results which I find tabled in my diary I humbly accept as the divine seal upon this special work which I had undertaken at what I then felt, but now know, was the call of God.

As my thoughts turn back to those busy but happy days, my heart overflows with gratitude and gladness, accompanied with a feeling of wonder that God should so bless and use a poor and unworthy instrument for the furtherance of His glory. To Him be all the praise !

A breakdown in health in 1879 led me, as I have already stated, to retire from business ; and feeling the excitement and strain of mission work too severe, to my great regret I was reluctantly compelled to do less and less, until I entirely gave it up. Although my health was restored in course of time, I had then become so interested in the work of the Local Preachers' Mutual Aid Association that I spent most of my leisure in preaching for, and advocating the claims of, this organization, travelling thousands of miles east, west, north and south. This is not what I had planned for the closing years of my life, yet I cannot but feel that my path has been ordered of the Lord, and in this as in every other step of my life I have endeavoured to follow the leadings of Providence.

CHAPTER X

FOREIGN TRAVEL

'Go far—too far you cannot, still the farther
The more experience finds you.'
Beaumont and Fletcher.

FOR many years I have travelled my native land, covering from ten to fifteen thousand miles per year, chiefly on business and deputation work. In this way I have made the acquaintance of most places of importance in the British Isles. But I had neither leisure nor means to gratify my desire to see the regions beyond until I was well advanced in life. My first journey to foreign parts was taken in 1892, when I joined the first Summer Party to Grindelwald in connexion with the Reunion of the Churches Conferences. The company consisted of about 130, and included, besides several of my own family, a number of Wesleyan ministers and personal friends.

There is an exhilarating excitement about one's first visit to a foreign land, and my interest in everything I saw never flagged from the moment I set my foot on Belgian soil at Ostend to the hour of my return. Reaching Berne about the middle of the second day of travel, we had our first enchanting view of the Alps from what is known as 'The Terrace.' The range of mountain monarchs in the distance, swathed in bluish haze, with their snowy peaks glistening in the noon sunshine, is a poem or a fairy-dream to the beholder when it first meets his gaze. There are certainly compensations for those who are not privileged to see such sights until they reach mature years, if there is any truth in the proverb, 'Those who live on the Alps never see them.' We unquestionably *did* see the beauties of the Bernese Oberland on that glorious day in June, and the vision can never fade from the memory. The 'Playground of Europe' has of recent years been rendered so accessible to the multitude that it would be too commonplace to indulge in a description of the fascinations of the country. The solemn avalanche, the chameleon colours of the giant peaks in the morning and evening sun-rays, the awesome glaciers and entrancing thals and dashing falls are too widely known now to need description.

In 1896 I realized the dream of my life when, with some members of my family, I was able to take an Eastern tour. Travelling across France, we joined the s.s. *Midnight Sun* at Marseilles. Passing Caprera, the scene of Garibaldi's exile; Corsica, the birthplace of Napoleon; Elba, whither he was banished, and Pozzuoli (the Puteoli of the Acts), the landing-place of Paul when journeying to Rome, we disembarked at Naples. Of course we were victimized by enterprising pedlars and pertinacious beggars. The great event of our brief visit to Naples was the trip to Pompeii, the city of the dead. To walk through the silent and ruined streets of this once fashionable but depraved resort of the ancient Romans is an experience of the intensest interest. The evidences of shameful luxury and the most debasing vice are everywhere apparent in this disinterred Sodom of Roman times.

Re-embarking, we continued our voyage through the Straits of Messina, the Adriatic Sea, the Corinthian Canal, arriving at Piraeus, where we landed for Athens and pictured to ourselves the visit of the great Apostle to Mars Hill, as narrated in Acts xvii. Constantinople and Asia Minor were taken in our tour, and everywhere we made the acquaintance of that striking devotee, the Mussulman, and witnessed in many places his devotions when the muezzin calls him to prayer from the minaret of the mosque five times a day. The exiled Apostle John was brought vividly to mind as we sailed close by Patmos. Passing the island of Cyprus on Sunday, we arrived at Jaffa the next day, where we disembarked and made our way through its narrow and crooked streets. To take a railway ticket from Jaffa to Jerusalem is a strange mixing of the ancient and modern. The journey of fifty-four miles is full of interest to the Bible student, the whole distance being studded with associations of sacred history. The first sight of the Holy City was impressive and sublime, and produced in me indescribable emotions of reverence mingled with delight. Our jehu from the station to the hotel madly shouted and yelled and flourished his whip as he furiously drove us through clouds of dust and crowds of pedestrians.

It is as unnecessary as it would be tedious to give a detailed account of all the wonderful and interesting sights of this tour, which have been so adequately described by the graphic pen of many a master in the art; but I may be allowed to touch lightly on some of my experiences and impressions. Not the least interesting spot in the Holy City is the Mosque of Omar, which is situated in a spacious area once occupied by Solomon's Temple. Here one requires an escort consisting of a Turkish gendarme and an official from the British Consulate. At this mosque we first encountered the regulation, enforced at all Mohammedan shrines and tombs, not without its humorous side, which prohibits entrance to the holy enclosure unless the boots are removed or a pair of sacred slippers fastened over them. Though one respects the reverence that is intended, there is a touch of drollery in the sight of a number of tourists each hunting in a heap of overshoes at the threshold for a pair which will completely cover his own footwear. The Mosque of Omar, 'the Dome of the Rock,' is almost entirely taken up with a projecting and shapeless stone which formed the summit of Mount Moriah, and is said to have been afterwards used as the altar of sacrifice by the Jewish priests. Anyhow, there is a hole bored through the rock which is supposed to have been used to drain off the blood of the victims. One has to receive a good deal that is said with the proverbial grain of salt ; as, for instance, when they gravely show you on this sacred rock the footprint of Mohammed and the impression of the hand of Gabriel the archangel ! All this is discreetly dealt with by Mark Twain in his *New Pilgrim's Progress*, a good companion on a journey through Palestine. The site of the ancient Holy of Holies is approximately indicated, and lies to the west of the Mosque. It is a spot still held by the Jews to be superlatively sacrosanct ; and at the hotel table I listened to a well-argued debate by residents in Jerusalem on the question whether the fact that Jews never enter the precincts of the old Temple is due to their forcible exclusion by their enemies the Turks or is a voluntary abstention on the ground that they might unwittingly commit the desecration of trespassing on the site of the Holiest Place. A visit to the Church of the Holy Sepulchre brings one face to face with the much-debated point as to whether the traditional site of Calvary, or the skull-like mound on the outside of the north wall, now known as 'Gordon's Calvary,' was the scene of the Crucifixion. A discussion by several D.D.'s and scholars, assembled at the latter site, inclined me to the view that Gordon's contention was reasonable. Perhaps there is divine wisdom in not allowing the Church to fix with certainty the exact locality of the greatest event in the world's history.

Our programme included a visit to Jericho, and the loneliness and roughness of the road helps one to understand the story of the Good Samaritan and to feel the force of the name by which it was known, at any rate as far back as the time of Jerome, viz. 'The Bloody Way.' The cry for 'baksheesh' greets the ear everywhere. Adults and children join in this perpetual demand. At Jericho, feeling sorry for some miserable-looking little Arabs who were raising the usual plaintive wail for baksheesh, I threw down a copper here and there, when one of them covered my hand with kisses, then a second kept kissing the other hand, and a third wished to kiss my face, but this honour I declined. Whether their attentions were those of disinterested affection, or spoke that kind of gratitude which is 'a lively sense of favours to come,' I am not prepared to decide. Of course our visit was not completed until we had bathed in the brackish waters of the Dead Sea and had had a dip in the River Jordan at the supposed spot where our Lord was baptized.

On visiting the Armenian Church in Jerusalem, the Patriarch, who lives there, honoured us with a reception in a large and handsome room. He chatted very freely, and entertained the party with 'Turkish delight' and water, and afterwards coffee, according to conventional custom. It was with deep feeling and a note of triumph in our voices that before leaving Jerusalem we gathered on the Mount of Olives and sang 'All hail the power of Jesu's name,' &c.

Egypt, our next objective, though not so sacredly classic as Syria, is in some respects a more pleasing country to visit. It is not under the rule of the 'unspeakable Turk,' and the benefits of British occupation are manifest on every hand. Alexandria, the place of landing, is not devoid of 'lions.' The railway journey to Cairo is a moving and wonder-provoking panorama to a Western unacquainted with mud villages except in pictures, or with trains of camels except in menageries, or with the picturesque dress and habits of the Egyptians in their native surroundings.

Cairo is one of the most cosmopolitan cities in the world. Western progress and Oriental conservatism meet and mingle in its streets. One is struck with the gross extravagance in expenditure on sumptuous shrines erected over the dead bodies of Mamelukes and Khedives. The monument to Ibrahim Pasha, which took seven years to build, is said to have cost £30,000. One of the most educational of the show places in Cairo is the Ghiza Museum, with its vast collection of relics going back to prehistoric Egypt. To a Bible reader, perhaps, there is nothing in the collection that produces such weird feelings as the mummied form of Rameses II, the Pharaoh of the oppression, with its magnificent physique and its finely chiselled and imperious features. The interior of

the Mosque El Azhar is one of the most sugges-
tive of the sights of this city. Here is a University
where 1,200 Mohammedan youths are drilled in
the knowledge of the Koran. Squatted on the
ground in groups around their teachers, they
commit to memory passages from their sacred
Koran, and are inspired with fanatical enthusiasm
for the honour of their great founder and the pro-
pagation of the doctrines of their cult. This they
do on the plainest and most meagre fare. Away
on the edge of the desert we were impressed with
the sight of those colossal erections, the Pyramids,
whose genesis and purpose are still wrapped in so
much mystery. Here, too, are some of the most
ancient buildings extant, preserved by drifts of
sand and excavated in recent years. Near Sakhara,
for instance, is the palace of Mera, with the colours
on its mural paintings quite fresh, although it
dates back some 5,300 years. In due course we
left this wonderful land of the Pharaohs and
returned to our own Land of Promise, thankful to
God for His goodness during our wanderings,
which covered 6,700 miles.

Two years later I undertook with my eldest son
a second tour in the East, covering somewhat
different ground. This time I had the opportunity
of making the acquaintance of Malta, full of
interest as the scene of Paul's shipwreck and of his
residence for three months. Here we encountered
the most terrifying hailstorm one can imagine,
with its hailstones scaling over a quarter of a

F

pound and doing enormous damage. Fortunately we were in a protected place, but it was easy to understand the deadly effects of the plague of hailstones, and the disaster to the Amorites when overtaken by such a storm as narrated in Joshua x. In Egypt our tour, though under different auspices, was pretty much a replica of the former visit. Our arrival in Palestine happened to synchronize with the visit of the German Emperor. On the afternoon of the Sunday which we spent in Jerusalem we had the unique privilege of attending an open-air service on Mount Olivet in company with the Kaiser and Kaiserin, and stood near those illustrious personages in the congregation. On this tour we travelled through the country from south to north on horseback, and in the wilds of northern Galilee nearly fell a prey to Bedouin highwaymen. Our route took us through Shechem, Samaria, Esdraelon, Nazareth, Cana, across the Lake of Gennesaret, over the shoulder of Hermon, and then to the oldest city of the world—Damascus—thence by way of Baalbek, with its majestic temple ruins, to Beyrout, where, taking the Messageries Maritime service, we sailed viâ Port Said and Alexandria to Marseilles, and so back to Old England.

Next in interest to my visits to the classic lands of the East, a tour which I was able to make through northern and mid Italy stands out in my foreign travel. In 1906, accompanied by my sons and son-in-law, I visited some of the famous places in this land of clear skies and light-hearted people.

Genoa, Rome, Naples, Capri, Pompeii and Vesuvius, Florence, Venice, and Milan were all included in the programme. Of this visit it would be easy to write at considerable length, but space forbids and necessity does not require it.

The following year a cruise in Norwegian seas afforded me the opportunity of acquainting myself with the rugged beauties of the fjords, into which the coast is broken, and of seeing something of the Scandinavian character and the simple and sombre habits of the people in the land of the Midnight Sun.

CHAPTER XI

BIRMINGHAM METHODISM

'We are conscious of being able to originate action,
To initiate events.'—*Illingworth.*

HAVING spent more than half a century of my life
in close and active connexion with Birmingham
Methodism, my autobiography would not be
complete without some reference to it. In the
year 1854 I settled in the metropolis of the
Midlands in the midst of a working-class popula-
tion. It was a crowded and not very salubrious part
of the town, surrounded by smoking chimneys and
gloomy factories where men and women worked
at occupations which rendered their appearance
anything but attractive. I acutely felt the change
in my environment, which contrasted harshly
with the rural beauties and charming scenery of
Sudbrook Park and Richmond. It would not be
an exaggeration to say that for some time I
hated the place. Neither did the condition of
Methodism in Birmingham at that time offer
any compensation for disagreeable material surroundings. My settlement in Birmingham occurred
only a few years subsequent to the distressing

Reform agitation, which had left its sears and scars on the Methodist life of the neighbourhood, so that I found the Church in an enfeebled and embarrassed state. Birmingham was at that date Methodistically divided into two Circuits, respectively called East and West, and my lot was to belong to the East Circuit, whose three principal chapels were burdened with debts amounting in the aggregate to £10,000. With few exceptions the membership consisted of men and women in humble life, who could render but little assistance towards lightening the heavy incubus resting on the trusts. In prosperous times, even with the aid of special effort, it was not easy to make both ends meet, and in bad times such as then existed trustees had to borrow money to meet current expenses. The outlook was gloomy; collapse, or bankruptcy in some cases, seemed inevitable.

When I became acquainted with the financial state of things I was greatly troubled, but had not the means to render any appreciable help. I fretted and prayed about the matter, which pressed heavily on my mind. During an alarming illness, with which I was prostrated, these church liabilities haunted me in my delirium. I was under the delusion that I was the victim of a diabolical plot to bury me alive, but on being conveyed to the place of interment it was discovered by some of my friends that I was not dead. I was released from the terrible doom awaiting me, and I commenced a law-suit and secured a verdict. The amount of damages awarded was fabulous. I scarcely knew how to dispose of the money, until the happy thought occurred to me that I would first of all liquidate all the chapel debts in the circuit. It was a ravishing thought, and ministered unspeakable delight, until consciousness returned, and I awoke and behold it was a dream.

After brooding over the difficulties for some time, the thought came to me that a division of the circuit would be a great advantage and possibly open the way for coping with the financial problems. I ventured to suggest that Belmont Row should be the head of one circuit and New Town Row the head of the other. Birmingham (West) had already been divided. My proposal was favourably entertained, and ultimately approved by the District Meeting and Conference. The Rev. H. M. Harvard, superintendent of the Belmont Row Circuit, proposed at the Quarterly Meeting that New Town Row section should raise a fund of £4,000, one half to reduce the debt on the New Town Row Chapel and the other half to build a new chapel at Lichfield Road. The development of this project is an interesting story, and as it fell to my lot to have a good deal to do with it I venture to narrate it here. A committee previously appointed to survey the new and growing district of Lichfield Road had reported failure in their efforts to find a place where Methodism might be started. Returning home from the meeting I remembered that at the back of a property in the neighbourhood, of which I happened to be agent, was a vacant workshop over a brewhouse that might provide accommodation for a time. Next day I reported this to the superintendent, who was much pleased with the proposal and said, 'I am just making the Circuit Plan and will put it on. Go and get it fitted up, and we will commence a Sunday school and preaching-service at once.' It proved to be a success, and before the circuit was actually divided, a plot of freehold land had been purchased, a school-chapel erected, and a scheme drafted for the building of a large chapel adjoining.

In submitting the scheme to the Circuit Quarterly Meeting, Mr. Harvard proposed that the £4,000 should be raised by subscriptions to be paid by instalments extending over five years, and appealed for promises ranging from £20 to £1 per year. This proposal did not seem to me to be bold enough, and I suggested the necessity of first securing promises of £100 and £50 per annum for the period named. Mr. Harvard was not sanguine about the possibility of this, and indeed no £100 offer was forthcoming, so that for a time the way seemed blocked. But God heard and answered prayer in a remarkable way. Just at that time the Birmingham Land Society, of which I was a director, acquired a building estate and appointed me with others to inspect the property and submit a plan for its development. I was responsible for the suggestion that instead of being cut up into small plots, as was customary, the estate should be disposed of in larger lots.   This unusual plan, though opposed by the chairman, was adopted by the Board.   Unfortunately on the day of the allocation it was found that no application whatever had been sent in for three of the largest fields, measuring about thirty-five acres.   Hitherto we had invariably received more applications for all land offered than we could meet, and the chairman twitted us with the failure of our new-fangled ideas.   I replied that I was sorry that my suggestion had not succeeded, and although I did not feel in a position to undertake such a large plot of land myself, rather than the reputation of the Society should suffer I would put in an application for it and trust to Providence.   Gratified at this solution they allotted the land in question to me. Before any instalment was due, a gentleman called at my office to ask if I would part with the land to him.   In reply to his question as to the amount of profit I wanted, I told him I should require £500. He demurred to my price, but subsequently called to accept the offer on my terms and laid down a cheque for the £500.   His name was substituted for mine at the Society's office and the transaction was completed.   I looked at the cheque and exclaimed to myself, 'What an extraordinary thing! I went into this matter contrary to my inclination, but am now quite out of it with £500 in pocket; what does it all mean?'   At last the truth dawned upon me, and I interpreted it as an interposition of Providence in answer to prayer. Hastening to the circuit steward's house, I announced to him that I had found one man who would contribute £100 per annum for five years to our Circuit scheme. Incredulous for a time, he at length asked doubtfully, 'Do you think he can be relied upon?' 'I think he can,' I replied. He was eager to find out who the donor was, but I kept him in suspense for a time, and finally in answer to his repeated inquiry, 'Who is it?' I said, 'I—and the Lord.' He became greatly excited, and said, 'Then I'll give £50 per year for five years,' and another friend who was present chimed in with equal ardour, 'And I'll do the same.'

From that time forward the friends in the Circuit became enthusiastic, and the scheme went like a prairie fire. The Rev. John Hearnshaw—a wonderful worker and beggar—was appointed to superintend the new circuit, and with his influence and help we met with unlooked-for success. To aid the effort a great bazaar was arranged, to be held in the Town Hall. As secretary I conceived several novel methods of helping the bazaar which proved very remunerative. One of these was a Bazaar Savings-bank, which was well pushed in the Sunday school and elsewhere. Attendance was given at a fixed time and place for the receipt of sums, large or small, with the understanding that 6*d.* would be added to every £1 paid in, and a free ticket of admission to the bazaar presented to each, together with vouchers, representing the amount deposited plus the bonus, which would be accepted as cash payment for goods purchased from the stalls. Another new idea that came to me as an inspiration was a lucrative mode of advertising the bazaar. It had been decided to issue 40,000 circulars, and it occurred to me that this might be made a valuable medium for trade advertisers. Waiting upon likely persons I offered a page in a small bazaar handbook for £5, which could be paid for in goods, and the goods, being sold in the bazaar, would further advertise the tradesman; or if he chose to pay in cash, a less sum was taken. A very liberal response was given, and the 40,000 programmes, publishing full details of the bazaar and its object, were distributed during an intervening holiday by the young men of the Improvement Class. By this means, beside a free advertisement of the bazaar, there resulted a gratifying profit to the funds, in cash and goods, of about £100. I believe I was thus the originator of the Bazaar Programme, which is now an almost invariable feature of bazaar arrangements.

But to complete the history of my donation of £500. I determined to invest the amount I had cleared in the land transaction referred to above, and meet my promise out of the proceeds. Taking a building lease of some land in the centre of Birmingham, I obtained plans for suitable premises, and the estimate for their erection was £500. Before the building was finished the premises were all let to substantial tenants at rents which yielded about

£150 per annum, after payment of ground rent; so that at the end of twelve months I was easily able to pay the first instalment towards the fulfilment of my promise. The Circuit scheme made such unexpected progress that it became possible to close it at the end of three years. In addition to paying off £2,000 from New Town Row debt, and building a chapel at Lichfield Road, three small chapels were erected and a minister's house furnished, and all in three years instead of five.

The Rev. H. M. Harvard, who was in the circuit at the time when the division was proposed, was a remarkable man. I owe an incalculable debt to him for his pastoral attentions, and his prayers for my recovery, during the most serious illness of my life, when death was hourly expected by doctors and friends. When Mr. Harvard called with his colleague to inquire how I was, he was told I was dying, which was no doubt perfectly true. He replied, 'Life is not gone yet; we can pray for him.' They retired with some members of my family to the drawing-room, and while they were pleading with God for my recovery a great change came over me. From that hour, to the astonishment of both physician and surgeon, I began to mend, and have since lived in fairly good health for over forty-five years. The medical men themselves regarded my recovery as a miracle, and to me it appears to be the clearest answer to prayer that ever came under my notice.

One of the saintliest and most gentlemanly men I ever met, Mr. Harvard was also immovable as a rock when he had once made up his mind. While invariably acting with extreme courtesy he insisted on having his own way. When calling on him to wish him farewell and to offer him a little token of my gratitude for his special kindness to me, I had the temerity to allow myself to be drawn out in some criticisms of his policy. I spoke frankly to him for about two hours and a half, during which time he listened with every attention and encouraged me to proceed from point to point; and at the close of the interview he said, 'I thank you very much, Mr. Barr; nobody has ever talked to me like this before. We have spent a very profitable morning.' At one of the Local Preachers' Meetings a brother asked why certain local preachers were planned at the large town chapels whilst others were systematically appointed only to the smaller places. This drew from Mr. Harvard the remark, 'I think you had better not press for an answer here; if you will see me privately I shall be pleased to tell you.' This did not pacify the questioner, who urged, 'I think it is a proper question for the Local Preachers' Meeting, and I shall be glad to have it answered.' 'Well then,' rejoined the Superintendent, 'the reason is that such brethren are unsuitable for the pulpits you refer to and the congregations do not want them. There are many circuits to which I should very much like to be appointed, but I never shall, for they will not have me.' That sufficed to close the conversation on that subject.

The great success of the New Town Row scheme acted as a stimulus and created holy rivalry in the sister circuit, whose people rose to the occasion and liquidated the debts on Belmont Row and Bradford Street Chapels. Birmingham Methodism grew financially much stronger, and has so far developed that where there were only two circuits there are now eight, not to mention the great Central Hall in Corporation Street which superseded old Cherry Street.

It may be of interest to my readers if I introduce to them one or two eccentric though saintly Methodists who at the time of which I have been writing belonged to the Birmingham (East) Circuit. Father Elwell was popularly known as the 'Bishop of Nechells.' He was a class-leader at Nechells Green Chapel, a plain and quaint brother, whose personality gave him prominence in the affairs of the Church. He exercised an authority which at times was somewhat despotic. Should a local preacher happen to enter the pulpit without donning a white neckerchief, if he did not have a bad time when preaching he would probably have one when he returned to the vestry, as the little man with his heavy-rimmed spectacles looked searchingly at his irreverent neck attire or at any other part of his get-up which did not conform to his strict and puritanical notions. Did an angry discussion break out at any meeting at which the 'Bishop' was present, or if anything out of place was spoken, he would rise to his feet, and with commanding voice and in staccato tones would say to the offender, 'Drap it!' the effect of which was usually electric. He was a devoted and efficient class-leader, and though an [unlettered man, preachers who rose to distinction—such as the Rev. Samuel Coley—were included amongst his members.

The mention of Mr. Coley recalls another brother of similar stamp who was in those days factotum at our little cause in the village of Coleshill. On one occasion Samuel Coley, a mere boy in round jacket, went as supply to this place. The brother referred to was in the vestry on the preacher's arrival. Eyeing his youthful appearance and dress, he asked, 'And what is your name, pray?' 'Samuel Coley,' was meekly returned. 'And who sent you?' was the next inquiry. 'The Rev. Mr. ——, the superintendent,' Samuel answered. 'Hm!' rejoined the man of years in discouraging tone, 'I thought some man sent you, for I felt sure God didn't!' Probably this unwise official lived to learn that the young beginner was, like his Old Testament namesake, called of God to prophesy.

Birmingham Methodism to-day will compare very favourably with the Methodism of fifty years ago. There are many more churches—more commodious, more attractive and in more conspicuous positions. We have a better-educated pulpit ministry. There is also a great deal of generous giving ; large sums of money are more easily raised than formerly; and there is a deeper interest in the social life not only of those inside, but of those outside the churches. Temperance reform, too, has taken a firmer hold of the Methodist community. I remember the time, since I went to live in Birmingham, when a Temperance Society or Band of Hope would be prohibited on certain Trust premises. For all these signs of progress I feel devoutly thankful; but if I were to be asked whether Methodism is in a more flourishing state spiritually, with profound regret I must give my opinion in the negative. The neglect of Class-meeting, Prayer-meeting, Lovefeast, and Band-meeting is to my mind not a hopeful sign. These things are significant of much. There seems to be less regard for family worship, Bible-reading, religious conversation and correspondence. Such exercises are apparently being supplanted by the drama, the dance, the card-table and trashy literature. The passion for pleasure is starving the spiritual life of many professing Christians. Alas, this state of things is not peculiar to Birmingham, nor to Methodism. There are lamentable indications that it is very general. No wonder that Church membership is suffering serious declension, and unless the Church is baptized afresh with the Holy Ghost it is to be feared that the more spiritual means of grace will entirely cease to exist. 'O come, great Spirit, come!'

CHAPTER XII

FILLONGLEY METHODISM

'And He went round about the villages teaching.'—*Mark* vi. 6.

IT goes without saying that the position of my own Church in my native parish lies very near to my heart. The last chapter presented a picture of Methodist expansion in a great city; I propose to devote this chapter to a narrative of the revival and re-establishment of Methodism in a rural district. It was here I received my natural birth, and in the little sanctuary, hard by my childhood's home, I received my spiritual birth. When quite a small boy I was taken by my mother to a religious service in the house of Father Price, an old, grey-headed, and toothless veteran, who sat in the meeting wearing a white night-cap, very lustily joining in the singing, and greatly enjoying the service. The little chapel must have been closed at the time. I believe it was originally built in 1828 by the Independent Methodists, who held service there for a short time until the cause failed and the place was shut up. At any rate, it was not in use as a place of worship in the year

[Photo by Pitt & Son, Worcester.

LOCAL PREACHERS' HOMES, FILLONGLEY

1837, at which date it was in the market and was about to be converted into a workshop. My father, though in humble circumstances and at that time unconverted, was much troubled, and felt it to be sacrilege to turn a house of prayer into a house of merchandise. He therefore went to the owner and bought the property, which included a cottage and garden adjoining. The chapel, together with a fair-sized plot of freehold land on either side, was valued at £60, so that it may be imagined it was an unpretentious structure. The building would certainly not accommodate more than one hundred hearers. There was a mortgage on the combined property, and my father acquired the equity of redemption at a cost of £54. How he raised this moderate sum of money I do not know.

Soon after the purchase was completed he consented to let the chapel to the Wesleyan Methodists for £3 per annum—5 per cent. on the £60 at which it was valued. It was put on the Plan of the Coventry Circuit, and preaching commenced. The pulpit was generally supplied by local preachers, many of whom had to trudge a distance of six and some of them eight or nine miles each way. The infrequent visits of the travelling preachers were usually on a week-night, on which occasions the quarterly tickets of the members were renewed or the Sacrament of the Lord's Supper administered. The cause was maintained with varying success for nearly forty years, until the death of my eldest brother in 1875. On his decease the little

G

place was sold by auction to a Birmingham tradesman who took no interest in Methodism; and
the few poor members, having no other place of
worship within reach, were obliged to attend the
parish church, a mile off. Among these was my
sister, a godly widow woman in humble life, who
begged me to exert myself to get Methodism
re-established in the village. I obtained from the
owner of the quondam Wesleyan Chapel the option
of purchase; whereupon I offered to make a gift of
it to the Coventry Circuit if they could supply it
with preachers. Presumably they felt themselves
unable to undertake to revive a feeble and distant
cause, for my offer was not accepted. I then sur-
rendered my option in favour of a Birmingham
solicitor, who bought it that his wife might carry
on there a Mothers' Meeting. I relinquished my
right to purchase on one condition. 'That little
chapel,' I told him, 'has been a great blessing to
me, and if the Methodists ever want to use it for
preaching you must let them have it.' 'I am a
Churchman,' he said, but intimated it would be all
right.

Though I was thwarted in my efforts, my sister
was still intensely eager to see Wesleyan Methodism
recommenced in the neighbourhood, and resolved
on a self-sacrificing effort to accomplish this. She
was taken ill about this time, and I went to see
her. I had no sooner reached her bedside than
she said to me, 'Talk about the little chapel.'

'Well,' I said, 'what can I do in the matter?

I offered to buy and give the old place to the Coventry Circuit, but they did not accept it, and now the chance is gone. The purchaser is dead, and I have been to his son, who disclaims any knowledge of his father's promise to me. He says he has given the use of it to the vicar for a mission service, and in the absence of anything in his father's handwriting to the contrary he will not comply with my request. If a new chapel could be built I know of no circuit that could work it.'

She replied with emphasis, 'I am here possibly on my deathbed, and I have promised God—circuit or no circuit—there shall be a Methodist chapel. I have saved £60, and with £25 of it I have bought a site for a new chapel in the village.'

She handed me her Savings-bank book, saying, 'Take that and begin with the £35 left.'

I expressed the opinion that she was not justified in parting with her savings. 'The money is not mine,' she protested, 'I have given it to the Lord.'

Deeply touched by her noble devotion, I resolved to do what I could to gratify her desire. I submitted the case to the Quarterly Meeting of the Islington Circuit, Birmingham, and secured the promise that if the chapel could be built and opened free of debt it should be put on the Plan, although it was far removed from the boundary of the circuit. My sister's heroic example soon became known and stirred up sympathy amongst friends in town. One lady on whom I called upon business, without any intention of asking help for the scheme, said, 'I have heard of the generous act of your sister, and am going to help; put me down for £50.' A few days later she said, 'Put the £50 down to my husband; I will lay a stone and give £20 more.' I had been thinking of a plain building to cost £300 or £400; but funds were supplied so freely we had enough to add a schoolroom and then a vestry to our plans. Still we found we had more than sufficient, and we decided on building a spire to the structure and erecting a caretaker's house with a suite of rooms for the use of preachers who preferred to go on Saturday and remain till Monday. At the last opening service it was found we had spent over £1,000, all of which amount was provided, with a small balance in hand. Finding that we required more land than my sister had bought, on application to Lord Leigh, the adjoining owner, his lordship graciously gave us all we wanted. Moreover, he laid one of the foundation-stones of the building, making a further contribution, giving a friendly and interesting address at the ceremony, and remaining afterwards to the tea-meeting.

My work in connexion with the Local Preachers' Mutual Aid Association has frequently occasioned me pain on account of certain cases of peculiar pathos which have come before us. It seemed to me that if some of these more destitute but deserving brethren could be further cared for by having a cottage and garden provided rent-free, it would

'INVERNESS'
(Author's Residence)

relieve them of anxiety and brighten the evening of their lives. Impressed with the idea, I bought a piece of freehold land in Fillongley, and, assisted by a number of friends, erected seven picturesque and comfortable cottages, at a cost, including land, of £1,650. The property was vested in twelve local Methodist gentlemen, half of whom happen to be Justices of the Peace. The trust now includes two houses subsequently built on the surplus land, freehold property in Lancashire and four additional cottages, which yield an income sufficient for the upkeep of the Cottage Homes and the supply of a small weekly allowance to the occupants. The trust-deed permits local preachers belonging to any of the Methodist Churches to occupy the Homes; and if any unforeseen difficulty arises the trustees have power to sell and devote part of the proceeds to the Local Preachers' Mutual Aid Association and the remainder for the furtherance of Methodism in Fillongley. The brethren living side by side help each other by fraternal fellowship and mutual attentions, enjoy pleasant intercourse in discussing questions of common interest, and aid one another in the upward and heavenly path. The Homes being situated close to the chapel, the inmates can easily attend the means of grace, while their presence and prayers prove an inspiration to the appointed preachers. It is a source of much gratification and thankfulness that I have been enabled to put a little sunshine into the eventide of worthy men, and their widows, who are permitted to remain in the Homes in case their husbands predecease them.

That this ministry of love is fully appreciated was attested when to my great surprise I was made, some time since, the recipient of a beautifully illuminated address couched in the following terms : 'We, the first occupiers of the Cottage Homes, Fillongley, desire to express our great thankfulness and indebtedness to you the promoter, and the trustees, for this noble institution. Now that the infirmity of years is upon us, we consider it to be a great boon to be so well provided for in our old age. Praying that the blessing of Almighty God may abundantly rest upon you, we remain, yours most gratefully.' Then follow the names of the seven brethren, with the date, August 7, 1889.

It is to me an unspeakable satisfaction to see in my native place the prettiest village chapel I have ever met with, and to witness Methodism so well established and with so good a prospect. To God be all the praise !

CHAPTER XIII

SHADOWS

'Shall we receive good at the hand of God, and shall we not receive evil?'—*Job.*

ALTHOUGH my life, now running out to the end, has been on the whole bright, joyous, and successful, it would not accord with universal experience were I able to claim that there had been no bitterness in my cup, no cloudy days, no dark and dreary nights. I have shared the common lot of men in this respect, and therefore feel it right to refer to a few of the chastening incidents of my life; otherwise my story might produce a wrong impression on the reader's mind.

For many years my father's family remained an unbroken circle. Death, the great Intruder, did not enter our home until I had grown to manhood. When about twenty years of age news was suddenly brought to me that my brother William, a healthy and stalwart farmer, had met his end through his foot slipping into a threshing-machine which was at work on his premises. It was a terrible shock, and but for the kind sympathy of my then master I felt that the blow would have been more than I could bear.   With a bleeding heart I followed my brother to the grave.   Oh, the pain and awe when death comes so close to one, and with such startling and tragic suddenness, for the first time!

A more distressing trial awaited me when I was called to the deathbed of my mother, whom I tenderly loved.   She left us on August 24, 1855, at the age of sixty-three.   Amongst her last words were these, 'I fear no condemnation; my Father's wrath is o'er.'   That happy testimony soothed my sorrow; but to say 'Good-bye' to one who was so sympathetic and loving, to whom I had so often gone for comfort, and not in vain, made a heart-wound which was not soon healed.

Sixteen years later my father was called Home, at the age of eighty-one.   Although the bond between us was not so strong as the maternal tie, he had uniformly toiled hard through a long life for the welfare of his children, and had done all in his power to further their interests.   His empty chair was to me the picture of desolation.   With a sorrowful heart we laid him in his last resting-place.   A regular worshipper at the little chapel, and greatly interested in the cause, he never became a member of the Church; and being extremely reticent on religious experience I could never get into close conversation with him as to his knowledge of the converting grace of Christ.   It was a great relief and satisfaction, therefore, to hear his dying testimony given in the familiar words of the Psalmist, 'Though I walk through the valley of the shadow

of death I fear no evil, for Thou art with me ; Thy
rod and Thy staff they comfort me.'

In November 1875 the news suddenly reached
me, near midnight, that my eldest brother was
dangerously ill and desired to see me. He lived
seventeen miles distant, but I had my horse put in
the conveyance and drove through the night with
all speed. I saw at once that he was marked to
fall, and indeed the end appeared to be very near.
In answer to my question if all was right with God
he said, 'That has long been a settled question,'
adding other words in confirmation. After a few
days he breathed his last, and we followed to the
grave one who, with bitter domestic sorrow, was
nevertheless an industrious, earnest, warm-hearted
Christian man, always ready to do a kind act, and
to render help to those in need to the utmost of
his ability.

The next heavy stroke came five years later,
when my youngest daughter succumbed to a mortal
malady from which she had suffered acutely for
many months.

The next to be taken from me was my loving
and faithful wife, who had been a comfort and brave
help-meet for about thirty years. After a long
period of suffering she triumphantly passed away
in 1885, on the anniversary of my birth. The
pang of parting was greatly relieved by her beautiful testimony. For a long time before the end
came, in spite of severe pain, her testimonies were
a means of grace to those who were in her room.

Death itself seemed to be robbed of all its terrors, and her chamber was like the vestibule of heaven.

My brother George fell asleep on his birthday, February 18, 1892. A local preacher and class-leader, he was a man of exemplary patience, gentleness of spirit, and uniform consistency of Christian conduct. I look back upon his life as a beautiful picture of the triumph of divine grace under heavy and prolonged trial.

Another sore affliction overtook me when the news arrived of the death of my second son in South Africa. Of exceptional gifts, he had made a successful start as an architect in Durban, with every prospect of a brilliant career in his profession, when an attack of appendicitis struck him down and carried him off in a few days, at the early age of twenty-nine. What such news means to a father only those can tell who have experienced the blow.

I think I have now finished my dolorous strain, but before closing the chapter I am constrained to acknowledge with profound gratitude the many compensations that I am able to set against the pathetic incidents on which I have only lightly touched.

The loneliness of my domestic life, which lasted for some years after the loss of my wife, was at length relieved when in 1889 I again married, my second wife being the widow of Mr. Martin Heath, of Crewe.

Surrounded in my old age by abundant mercies I await the call that shall summon me to 'my Father's House on high.'

CHAPTER XIV

CLOSING REFLECTIONS

'Does the road wind up-hill all the way?
  Yes, to the very end.
  Will the day's journey take the whole long day?
  From morn to night, my friend.'
Christina Rossetti.

IN reviewing the past and going over many pleasing reminiscences, I am overwhelmed with a deep sense of God's abounding lovingkindness to me through a long life. 'Bless the Lord, O my soul, and all that is within me, bless His holy name.' Though keenly conscious of frequent mistakes and shortcomings, for sixty-seven years I have been kept in the narrow way, have still a good hope through grace, and am to-day travelling onward, upward, homeward, heavenward. Many who started life with me, having better prospects, have made shipwreck of body and soul, and have gone to a dishonoured grave. Drink and vice have hastened the end of some of my early acquaintance. One who accompanied me the first day I went to school committed a crime and was sent, disgraced, a convict to a penal settlement. Some with fairer worldly prospects have been reduced to beggary, and some have filled paupers' graves. God has favoured me with increasing prosperity; I have every happiness and comfort in my home, with enough and to spare of this world's goods, affectionate children united in the closest bonds and all walking in the fear of God. What more could I desire or possess to complete my happiness?

With those in mind who are commencing life and wish to make it a success, I will close this narrative by mentioning a few things which helped me in my early struggles, and which if carefully observed will be of equal service to others.

1. RELIGION.—I cannot exaggerate the advantages that have come to me through commencing my religious life in early years. I have realized the truth of the words, 'Godliness is profitable unto all things, having promise of the life that now is as well as of that which is to come.' I greatly pity those who sneer at religion. Genuine piety restrains from those things which inevitably pull men downward; it inculcates habits of industry, thrift, economy and prudence, and these are essential to material success in life. It gives character, and that commands respect from those who have no regard for religion. I have, throughout my career, sought divine guidance and watched for the moving of the pillar of cloud, and have often proved the wisdom of the counsel, ' In all thy ways acknowledge Him, and He will direct thy paths.'

'AT HOME'

2. TOTAL ABSTINENCE.—Abstinence from intoxicants has not only been a safeguard from perils that have ruined many, but has in various ways been of immense assistance to me in my efforts to succeed in life, not to mention the leverage it has given me in such Christian service as I have been able to render.

3. CHURCH MEMBERSHIP.—The fellowship of the Methodist Class-meeting I have found to be a great help and stay, and a blessing to me temporally as well as spiritually. The remembrance of my Church membership has steadied me in temptation, and the influence of its fellowship has inspired me with fortitude and courage. Indeed I have the conviction that but for the benefits of the Class-meeting I should have gone back into the world.

The catalogue of the primary forces that have contributed to any success that I have achieved would not be complete if I did not give a prominent place to the influence upon me through life of a godly mother. Her hand has powerfully worked in the shaping of my character and destiny. It is more than half a century since we laid her in the grave; but I feel the touch of her loving hand on my head yet, and still hear her tender voice speaking to me. I have never lost the charm and spell of her influence, which even now makes it difficult if not impossible to do anything I know she would not approve. Her saintly example still lives before me, and operates as a controlling force in my life.

I cannot conclude this brief account of my life more fittingly than in the language of the Psalmist:

'BLESS THE LORD, O MY SOUL,
AND FORGET NOT ALL HIS BENEFITS:
WHO FORGIVETH ALL THINE INIQUITIES;
WHO HEALETH ALL THY DISEASES;
WHO REDEEMETH THY LIFE FROM DESTRUCTION;
WHO CROWNETH THEE WITH LOVINGKINDNESS AND
    TENDER MERCIES;
WHO SATISFIETH THY MOUTH WITH GOOD THINGS;
SO THAT THY YOUTH IS RENEWED LIKE THE EAGLE'S'

CHAPTER XV

CLOSING SCENES

BY REV. D. W. BARR

' God's finger touched him and he slept.'—In Memoriam.

THE preceding narrative was written during the closing year of the author's life. About the time that he first put pen to paper an insidious disease suddenly revealed itself. He had been making notes for his life-story; and now he felt that if it was to be written no time must be lost. With characteristic determination he set himself to what he feared might be his last task. When it was finished and in the publisher's hands his strength had seriously declined. The proof-sheets were read in his sick room. He earnestly hoped that he might live to see the little book issued from the press; but this was not to be. Before the final proof was received—indeed the very morning it arrived—the messenger of heaven reached him.

The writer's sole object in this autobiography was to do good. Unable during the last year of his life to preach, he desired that, if possible, his pen should speak for the Master. We who are charged with the sacred task of executing his

wishes send forth this modest volume in the prayer-
ful hope that through it "he being dead may yet
speak.' Its pages breathe the Psalmist's spirit :
' Come and hear, all ye that fear God, and I will
declare what He hath done for my soul.'

The last illness was peculiarly chastening to one
who retained to the end an unabated spirit of
indomitable activity. Happily there was no acute
physical suffering ; but the prospect of distressing
developments was continually before him and his
family. Gradually the bodily powers failed, and
he resigned himself to the inevitable. The strong
faith that had been his mainstay throughout life
sustained him during this trying period. He spoke
confidently about the future to the members of his
family and the many friends who visited his sick
room. There lies before me his rough copy of one
of the last letters he penned, which exhibits his frame
of mind at this time, and I therefore transcribe a
portion of it. It was written in bed to the veteran
local preachers in the Fillongley Cottage Homes
which he was mainly instrumental in founding.

' My beloved Friends,
        ' I think the time is very near when I
shall be leaving you, and must take my last farewell till we meet in the Better Land. . . . Some
of you will soon be following me, and we shall then
be "for ever with the Lord "—free from all pain
and sorrow. "O what a joyful meeting there !"
I feel that the old gospel, which we have been

permitted to preach for so many years, will not fail me now; it is my strength and stay, the one and only foundation—a rock " sure and steadfast."

'May God's richest blessing be abundantly vouchsafed to every one of you. What a grand inexhaustible treasury of grace is open to us! O that we all more thoroughly realized this, and lived up to the full enjoyment of our privileges. My regret is that I have only had a few drops from the river of life when I might have bathed in the full ocean of the great Redeemer's love. I feel that I have been an unfaithful and unprofitable servant—

> A poor sinner, and nothing at all,
> But Jesus Christ is my all in all.

To His boundless mercy and grace I owe it all. . . .

'I hope you may all be spared as much suffering and sorrow as is consistent with your heavenly Father's will, and that you may have a bright and happy eventide. . . .

'I should like to have written you a longer and more interesting letter, but I feel too feeble and worn for the effort.

'With very affectionate regards to all, and commending you each to the loving care of your heavenly Father,

'I remain, your brother in Christ,

'DAVID BARR.'

The following facts will help to complete the author's own narrative. The last sermon he preached was at Raunds, Northampton, on February 7, 1909, the text being characteristic of his pulpit ministry: 'Testifying both to Jews and to Greeks repentance toward God and faith toward our Lord Jesus Christ' (Acts xx. 21). From his sermon register it appears that at each of the two services taken by him that day he had a 'good time.' Thereafter he was unable to conduct public service owing to permanent loss of voice. He continued his active duties more or less to within a few weeks of the end. He was present at the Covenant Service on the first Sunday of this year, when he partook of the Communion for the last time, though even so late as the Saturday previous to his death he expressed the hope that he might again join in the fellowship of the Lord's Table with the members of the Church. The summons came in the early morning of Wednesday, March 9, 1910, and he entered the eternal light, peacefully and without a struggle, nine days before the seventy-ninth anniversary of his birth. For wellnigh sixty years he had been 'preaching peace by Jesus Christ' with great ardour and not a little success, and in the passing of his soul across 'the narrow stream of death' the Master calmed His servant with His 'Peace, be still!'

The respect in which he was held was witnessed by the large attendance at his funeral, which included representatives from both religious and commercial circles. He was interred at the General Cemetery, Birmingham, on Saturday, March 12.

The beautiful service at Sandon Road Wesleyan Church, preceding the interment, gathered no gloom about it. The Rev. R. A. Mitcheson Brown, who had been in close and constant pastoral intercourse with the departed throughout his illness, presented a life-like portraiture of his character. I may appropriately conclude this chapter with a summary of his address :

'We meet to-day to thank God for the gift of a good man, who fulfilled his days, wrought valiantly and successfully through a long and arduous life, and in a mellow age passed to his reward. So our grief is not gloom, it is not even grey ; it is iridescent, shot through with the light of immortality and eternal life ; our tears are sun-kissed. By his sleepless energy, toil, and ability our departed friend won for himself positions of honour and trust in commercial and civic life. He was converted to God when twelve years of age through the preaching of Thomas Collins, but he always acknowledged his great debt to the heroic character and gracious influence of his mother. He began to preach at the age of twenty. Like his spiritual father, he was thoroughly evangelical in his spirit and preaching. He laboured for souls, and, especially in earlier days, saw many gathered into the Church under his ministry. He was a loyal Methodist, serving his Church with singleness of heart, holding nearly every office open to a layman. His sympathies were with the best side of our

Methodist life, and he was a stalwart defender of our more spiritual institutions and traditions. He told me more than once that he was naturally pessimistic, but that lately he had seen many signs that cheered his eventide; the clouds were lifting, and he felt sure the sun would shine. He was an old-fashioned Methodist, a man of strong convictions, and held them very tenaciously. He loved work, revelled in it; he enjoyed life, and was not eager to quit it. When a malignant disease made preaching impossible, he bravely continued many forms of work until absolutely compelled to relinquish them. Those of us who were privileged to visit him will never forget the ministry of those last weeks. He was happy with his family about him, happy in their ceaseless and affectionate tendance, happy in freedom from great pain, most of all happy in his heart. The religion he had preached and practised served him to the end. He had no misgivings about his spiritual state; again and again he spoke of rest, confidence, assurance. He met death with fortitude and the serenity born of a perfect trust. The chamber where he slept away to God was a veritable vestibule of heaven. His favourite word for the Beyond was " Home," and his passing has been a triumph, an ascension, a coronation.'

March 31, 1910.

R. Clay & Sons, Ltd., London and Bungay.

www.ingramcontent.com/pod-product-compliance
Lightning Source LLC
LaVergne TN
LVHW081346060426
835508LV00017B/1435